Striving Together

Striving Together

Early Lessons in
Achieving Collective Impact in Education

Jeff Edmondson

and

Nancy L. Zimpher

Foreword by

Ben Hecht

Published by State University of New York Press, Albany

Printed in the United States of America

For information, contact State University of New York Press, Albany, NY
www.sunypress.edu

Production, Ryan Morris
Marketing, Michael Campochiaro

Library of Congress Cataloging-in-Publication Data

Striving Together: Early Lessons in Achieving Collective Impact in Education /
    Jeff Edmondson, Nancy L. Zimpher; foreword by Ben Hecht.
    ISBN 978-1-4384-5605-8 (hc : alk. paper)
    ISBN 978-1-4384-5604-1 (pbk. : alk. paper)
    E-ISBN 978-1-4384-5606-5 (ebook)

2014941976

10 9 8 7 6 5 4 3 2 1

Jeff:
To Kelly and my kids, Emmy, Isabel, Alex, and Maddie.
Your constant love and support—
particularly your patience when I am on the road—
has sustained me every step of the way on this ongoing journey.

Nancy:
To children and grandchildren everywhere,
whose collective future is at the center of this work.

Contents

Part III. Creating a Community of Practice

Foreword

Ben Hecht

In July 2007, I was invited by the Brookings Institution to attend the Global Urban Summit, held at the Rockefeller Foundation's conference center on Lake Como in Bellagio, Italy. At the time, I was about to start a new job as president and CEO of Living Cities, a philanthropic collaborative of 22 foundations and financial institutions dedicated to bringing about transformational change for low-income urban Americans. I looked forward to connecting with leaders doing groundbreaking work in urban settings, in large part because I was in the market for ideas with the potential to improve the lives of millions of Americans.

I had been working in the social change field for more than 20 years, in several different capacities and sectors: higher education, nonprofit, and philanthropic. I had seen many great individual programs and worked with amazing, charismatic leaders, public and private. What I hadn't seen, however, was needle-moving impact: millions of lives changed, not just thousands. I had come to realize that innovative programs, no matter how effective, could never overcome dysfunctional systems. If we didn't attack and fundamentally change the systems, then we would never get desired and sustained results.

There were indeed many innovative organizations and ideas represented at the Brookings convening. But one leader arrived in Bellagio armed with a vision—and a project on the ground—that felt suspiciously like the transformative approach to systems change I had been seeking.

That leader was University of Cincinnati president Nancy Zimpher, and her initiative was the StrivePartnership.

When Nancy told me about an effort in Cincinnati that she was a part of to transform educational outcomes, not just fix an underperforming program, I was intrigued. When she told me that the effort was being led by all the people who were running and funding the current dysfunctional system, I knew this had a real chance to be something important.

As she described the work, I knew that I had found a kindred spirit in Nancy. We shared a passion for systemic change and an understanding that unless we radically reform the way we deliver services, we won't get the job done. Like me, she was committed to dramatically picking up the pace and scale of positive social change.

As Nancy told me about this new cross-sector collaborative, we were looking over one of the most scenic views in the world. But later that evening in my hotel, as I read more about the StrivePartnership, the ideas and process were just as compelling, even without the spectacular backdrop.

What I read confirmed my gut reaction: That it represented an unprecedented opportunity to tear down the silos where organizations get fixated on one aspect of a problem rather than working systemically. Moreover, this new configuration of leaders seemed to be creating just the type of new civic infrastructure that communities needed to keep the right people at the right table long enough to make a difference.

After Bellagio, when Living Cities staff traveled to Cincinnati and experienced the StrivePartnership leadership table firsthand, we had even more enthusiasm about supporting the effort. We wanted to help solidify the Framework and increase the chances that it could be adopted and adapted anywhere in the country.

What set this effort apart, from Living Cities' perspective, was the way that the table had been set with leaders who were willing to use their actual and implied authority as well as their political capital to get the work done. The participants had also agreed on the specific outcomes they wanted to change, and they had committed to using data to measure their progress, to hold *themselves* accountable.

And their core of chief executive-level leaders positioned them for success: Alongside Nancy Zimpher were KnowledgeWorks Foundation CEO

Chad Wick, Greater Cincinnati Foundation CEO Kathy Merchant, and local United Way president Rob Reifsnyder. The team's magical synergy of complementary skills and networks allowed them to recruit others through an unlikely combination of audacity, humility, and transparency.

Living Cities decided to invest, first with seed money to Knowledge-Works Foundation to begin distilling the approach into a framework that others could emulate, followed by a grant competition for communities to pilot the Framework. Through the grant we funded five sites, four of which are profiled in this book.

One of the biggest wins with the StriveTogether Framework was that it ultimately took very little money to begin scaling up. I believe this is because of the power of the idea, and a growing hunger and urgency among leaders across the country to break the stagnation. This, in combination with effective use of social media, helped bring about a remarkable explosion in interest and participation on a national level.

Of course, none of this scale-up would have been possible without the dogged determination and articulate vision embodied by Jeff Edmondson. As executive director of the original StrivePartnership of Cincinnati/Northern Kentucky, and now StriveTogether's managing director, Jeff has been a charismatic spokesman for this work. His commitment to cultivating the strength of the network and the rigor of its collective impact approach has been extraordinarily effective.

Nancy has continued to be a driving force in what we now call StriveTogether. As chancellor of the State University of New York's 64-campus system, she has been a champion and a sponsor of cradle-to-career networks on the local, state, and national levels.

Living Cities has not only invested in the scaling and development of the StriveTogether Framework; we have incorporated it into our work in every programmatic area, focusing on three critical elements: shared vision, articulated metrics, and a cross-sector table of executives who use data on progress to hold themselves and each other accountable. The Framework has served as a powerful structure for our Integration Initiative, which is supporting five cities to engage in a range of system-level changes that benefit low-income people.

As both a participant and an observer in the networks and replication that is taking place across the nation, I believe we are in the midst of a pivotal moment in which collaboration is becoming the new competition. Every day I encounter more leaders who understand the power and efficacy of these collaboratives and want to be a part of them.

StriveTogether's pioneering genius played a central role in this culture shift, and I could not be more proud to be a part of it.

We are still far from declaring victory on our goals of social and economic equity. But the rapid spread of this transformative way of doing business extends a singularly bright and hopeful light to the world, and the experiences detailed in these pages offer an indispensable blueprint for those ready to join this cultural vanguard. In my view, StriveTogether's cradle-to-career Framework is, hands down, our best bet to build a society where every child, every family, and every neighborhood can truly thrive.

Acknowledgments

Because our subject is collective impact work, we are blessed with an impossibly long list of partners, colleagues, investors, mentors, and co-conspirators without whom this story would never have taken place.

KnowledgeWorks Foundation (KWF) has been at the very center of this work since its inception, by providing the patient capital needed to let the partnership emerge locally and then supporting the national expansion. The ongoing positive influence of KWF's board of directors on this work cannot be overstated. Its members have persisted in serving up support, wisdom, and critical troubleshooting that have in large measure made this story possible. Our deepest appreciation goes to former board chair Joe Tomain for being a key "early adopter," support that has continued with current chair John Dean.

Ken Howey has worked closely with us from the first conversations, advising on issues around teacher preparation, pedagogy, and the needs of urban school districts. He also played a critical role in the development of the case studies in this book, visiting the sites, interviewing partners and staff, and synthesizing the experiences as lessons learned across the StriveTogether Network.

Chad Wick, former president and CEO of KnowledgeWorks, was and continues to be a great champion. His relentless pursuit of partners and boundless enthusiasm put this effort on solid ground, enabling the work to take root. Chad remains an active part of the network as CEO emeritus and a member of KWF's board of directors. Chad's successor, Judy Peppler, has also been stalwart in her support on behalf of KnowledgeWorks.

As executive director of the StrivePartnership, Greg Landsman has been a steady hand in continuously improving the local work in Cincinnati and Northern Kentucky, as well as making major contributions to the national conversation with his colleagues in sites across the nation. Greg has an excellent partner in Nancy Swanson, who has provided impeccable organizational leadership on behalf of Procter & Gamble as chair of the Partnership's executive committee.

The names "Kathy" and "Rob" appear frequently in these pages, referring to original champions and partners Kathy Merchant and Rob Reifsnyder. Kathy's willingness to bring the Greater Cincinnati Foundation to the table added fuel to Chad's fire as a boundary spanner between schools and communities. Rob's experience leading the United Way of Greater Cincinnati gave him a keen sense of both the challenges and the possibilities of coordinating the work of community-based organizations. His early advocacy of data-informed work helped push us in the direction of a strong evidence base. Both Kathy and Rob continue to serve a vital role in the evolution of cradle-to-career partnerships as members of the StriveTogether National Advisory Board.

One of the earliest glimpses of success came with the sign-on of Xavier University president Father Michael Graham and Jim Votruba, the former president of Northern Kentucky University. Our gratitude also goes out to Jim's successor, Geoff Mearns, and current University of Cincinnati president Santa Ono, both of whom champion the StrivePartnership today as members of its executive committee.

We're also grateful for Larry Johnson, then dean of University of Cincinnati's College of Education, Criminal Justice, and Human Services, who—along with a great team of UC graduate students—created the original Roadmap to Success. Other colleagues in higher education have continued to amplify the work in Cincinnati and Northern Kentucky: Ron Wright, former Cincinnati State president, and his successors John Henderson and O'dell Owens; and Ed Hughes, president of Gateway Community and Tech College.

The strongly unified support from higher education helped leverage regional K–12 leaders, giving us a clear shot at improving local education outcomes. Our deepest appreciation goes to former superintendents Rosa Blackwell (Cincinnati), Mike Brandt (Newport), and Lynda Jackson (Covington). Current superintendents Mary Ronan (Cincinnati), Kelly Middleton (Newport), and Alvin Garrison (Covington) continue as part of the StrivePartnership table.

Elected school board leaders have also been pivotal to the Strive-Partnership's success, particularly former Cincinnati Public Schools board chair Eileen Cooper-Reid and current chair Eve Bolton. The Cincinnati Federation of Teachers has also been an integral partner throughout this journey, starting with former presidents Sue Taylor and Tim Krause and continuing today with Julie Sellers, who is deeply committed to personalized learning for every child.

Early on in this journey we were fortunate to have broad and deep support from investors willing to go out on a limb to build capacity. Catalytic support from Ben Hecht and Living Cities—armed with Marian Urquilla's vision for replication—propelled the creation of the StriveTogether Framework and the original proof point sites. Joe Danek, who at the time coordinated the Coalition of Urban Serving Universities, worked closely with member campuses and Living Cities to get those first sites established.

Locally, the Carol Ann and Ralph V. Haile, Jr./U.S. Bank Foundation provided energy and investment at a critical early juncture when we needed to get the messaging right, carried forward by Leslie Maloney, an invaluable supporter of the StrivePartnership to this day as a member of the National Advisory Board.

We also benefited from early vision in how to take continuous improvement to scale in a community, using data to have greater impact. Procter & Gamble executive Jim Bechtold was a key visionary, along with Sean Parker who helped sustain support for the work. They engaged another corporate partner in General Electric Aviation, with Paula Kollstedt and then Pat Zerbe fully embracing the work.

FSG's John Kania and Mark Kramer saw something special in the StrivePartnership as they scanned the horizon for promising examples of systemic reform. Their groundbreaking 2011 research put our work on the map, unleashing a new wave of interest and awareness. It also positioned the effort in Cincinnati/Northern Kentucky as ground zero for the collective impact theory that emanated from their original *Stanford Social Innovation Review* article. Articulating the promise of this new way of doing business helped to spark a national movement, and for this they have our profound thanks and admiration.

The scale-up of the StrivePartnership that led to the creation of the national Cradle to Career Network was possible thanks to the leadership and talent of the members of the StriveTogether National Advisory Board, who continue to provide invaluable guidance, visibility, and sensible governance. The network would not have reached its current success without the commitment of such steadfast champions as Sue Lehmann, Stacey Stewart, Lance Fors, and Michelle Jolin, all of whom have connected critical dots and made the case for collective impact work nationally.

The Annie E. Casey Foundation continues as a philanthropic Hercules for the development of cradle-to-career partnerships, thanks to the dedication of president and CEO Patrick McCarthy, along with Donna Stark, Barbara Squires, and Sophie Dagenais. We've also benefited greatly from the diverse experiences and know-how of the entire 2010–2011 class of Annie E. Casey Foundation Children and Family Fellows, of which Jeff was a member.

Jeannie Oakes and Doug Wood at the Ford Foundation are extraordinary allies whose insights on education reform and social change have helped us bring greater rigor and quality to the StriveTogether Network. Rick Love has also provided substantial support on behalf of the MetLife Foundation, helping us gain traction early with a broader set of partners.

We are beyond grateful to the partners in the communities that pioneered this work whose stories grace these pages with valuable lessons learned: Dan Ryan and Nate Waas Shull in Portland, Bev Warren and Kelli Parmley in Richmond, Mary Jean Ryan and Lynda Peterson in Seattle, and Bob Wimpelberg and Donna Scott in Houston. We also thank every partner, cat-herder, staff member, and community member at sites coast to coast for devoting untold energy, political capital, and genius toward moving the dials.

This book had its own "backbone" in the form of Nancy's team at SUNY. Our thanks to Jessica Neidl for dedicating her remarkable research and writing skills to this effort. Casey Vattimo and Juliette Price also made significant contributions and kept the project moving forward. Alice Oldfather, Nancy's former editor at SUNY, came in as our own cat-herder to bring the project to fruition. Her ability to bring a range of ideas together into a common voice is second to none.

Jeff's staff in Cincinnati has also provided much-needed support along the way—particularly Damian Hoskins, who created many of the illustrations. Jennifer Blatz gave critical input, along with Carly Rospert and Jennifer Perkins. Linda Brandin is an invaluable partner who helps keep the trains running on time.

Our hats are off to State University of New York Press and its outstanding leaders, James Peltz and Donna Dixon, for their patient, abiding support and guidance of this project.

Finally, none of this work would have been possible without the children whose collective future is at the center of our work. They inspire us to keep digging deeper, to bring what works to scale.

Introduction

In 2006, a group of local leaders in Cincinnati came together for a town hall–style meeting to discuss a new college readiness program for low-income students. After much discussion, one of the participants, a county coroner, stood up and said, "As long as we remain program rich and system poor, we will not get more kids into college. And what's more, I'm going to continue to see dead kids on my table." The room resonated with the stark sense of truth and urgency in the statement. There it was. We weren't going to be able to program our way to better outcomes. We needed to find a new way of doing business.

This pivotal meeting amplified the concern among many of us that focusing on college access was not enough—that, in order to truly move the needle on educational outcomes in the region, we needed to go much bigger by aiming for the *systemic* change needed to transform children's lives.

After more meetings with a growing and diverse collaborative of leaders, a new approach to social change was born. Beginning as a partnership including three school districts in Cincinnati/Northern Kentucky, these leaders set out to improve educational outcomes in the urban core of the region, not by starting new initiatives, but instead by scaling local practices that were already getting results for kids and building a stronger "civic infrastructure," which we have come to define as

> The way in which a region or community comes together to hold itself collectively accountable for implementing their own unique cradle-to-career vision, and organizes itself to identify what gets results for children; improves and builds upon those efforts over time; and invests the community's resources differently to increase impact.[1]

1

Seven years later, the StrivePartnership of Cincinnati/Northern Kentucky has measured remarkable results: The region has seen a 13-percentage-point shift in the number of outcomes trending positively, including a nine percent increase in kindergarten readiness over four years across the three impacted cities of Cincinnati, Newport, and Covington. And today, the Partnership has given rise to StriveTogether, a growing national network of cradle-to-career partnerships across the United States.

But that is truly the "long story short" of this full-length version of this narrative. It needs to be said up front that we are true believers in this work. Having been involved since the very beginning, we have both seen the impact the StriveTogether Framework can have on a community. Now, with the viral surge in replication of the Framework and its emerg-

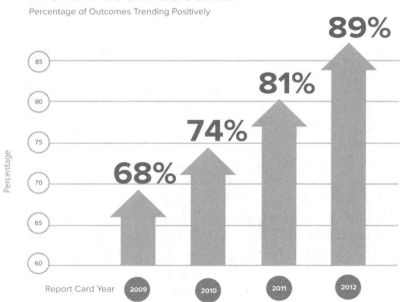

ing Theory of Action, we decided the time was ripe to provide a detailed look at how StrivePartnership and the StriveTogether Network came to be. The desire to share success stories and lessons learned, warts and all, grows out of a fundamental commitment in this work to accountability, transparency, and continuous improvement. It also reflects our dedication to cultivate a strong community of practice, one that functions like a healthy ecosystem with effective feedback and adaptation mechanisms. This is not easily achieved, as will be made clear in these pages.

And this is also a story about quality, about the very real challenge of bringing discipline and rigor to the social sector. It's about acknowledging how hard it is to get people to work together who are often separated into silos. It is about using data consistently not as a hammer but as a flashlight to help us figure out how to make smarter investments. We have been riveted on bringing the discipline Jim Collins spoke about in his monograph, *Good to Great for the Social Sector*. "A culture of discipline," Collins wrote, "is not a principle of business; it is a principle of greatness."[2] And perhaps most important, it is about being willing to "fail forward": to make mistakes along the way, be transparent about what was learned, and make adjustments at the local and national levels.

The fact that we—Nancy and Jeff—came to this work from very different pathways is also reflective of the critical importance of bringing rigor and discipline to this work across sectors. Nancy's journey began when she was a newly minted teacher, working in a one-room country school in the Ozarks, teaching four grades all subjects. It didn't take long for her to recognize where teacher training fell short in preparing her for this responsibility, and it was only a matter of time before she decided she wanted to teach teachers for classroom readiness. This decision led her to an academic career focused on improved teacher training.

As a faculty member at the Ohio State University directing undergraduate teacher education programs, Nancy took seriously the clarion call of the Holmes Group, a consortium of education deans and chief academic officers dedicated to improving the quality of teacher education programs. Later, when the group evolved into the Holmes Partnership—reflecting an evolving understanding that teacher education reform would require systemic partnerships with schools, school district administrators, and teacher leaders—Nancy assumed the organization's presidency.

During this time she put this commitment into practice by working directly with the Columbus Public Schools and the Columbus Education Association (the teacher's union) toward a deeper understanding of how key stakeholders need to work together on education reform. Here Nancy experienced firsthand the need for chief executives of all entities (in this case, the superintendent of schools and the president of the university) to be fully engaged and supportive of educational reforms.

She had this level of engagement in mind when she took the chancellorship of the University of Wisconsin-Milwaukee, where she led a strategic plan that resulted in a community partnership between UWM and the Milwaukee Public Schools to improve teacher education. Later, when Nancy moved back to Ohio to lead the University of Cincinnati, she again developed a strategic plan that included a major initiative to collaboratively improve outcomes for the Cincinnati Public Schools and the university, focused on college access.

This initiative led her into conversations with Chad Wick—then CEO of the KnowledgeWorks Foundation (where Jeff was serving as chief of staff)—and the beginning of a partnership that ultimately led to the creation of the StrivePartnership.

The seeds of Jeff's passion for system change were planted while he served as a Peace Corps volunteer. Stationed in Gabon, Central Africa, Jeff saw firsthand the dangers of overlaying generic solutions with no grounding in local reality. In neighboring Congo, fish farming had been implemented to address undernourishment brought about by overpopulation. Knowing little about the two countries outside of their proximity, a program administrator in D.C. assumed the same solution would apply in Gabon. The problem was, Gabon is comprised of 80 percent rainforest. If you want fish, all you have to do is to put a trap in the water.

Seeing the disconnect, Jeff stayed an extra year and a half to focus the fish-farming program on animal husbandry, a strategy that worked well with the circumstances on the ground. The experience demonstrated powerfully that unless you deeply understand the problem—and local needs—you cannot design solutions.

After the Peace Corps, Jeff worked at Washington, D.C.'s largest public high school, where he oversaw the interface between the school and resources within the community. In this role, he witnessed the extreme lack of coordination and accurate data available to make sound decisions and get good outcomes. Subsequent work in both public policy and philanthropy convinced Jeff that lasting change lay not in the hands of one sector or another but in leveraging each of their respective strengths. This conviction led him to KnowledgeWorks, a foundation focused on systems change and building civic capacity.

In 2005, our two very different pathways converged, a meeting of the minds that has produced a wonderfully productive partnership where we continue to learn from each other and make each other's contributions stronger. At the outset of our relationship, we had each just taken our place at the remarkable leadership table in Cincinnati. And as we looked around at what began to emerge, we both recognized that the group of leaders who had assembled had the potential to transform the landscape of social and educational change in our community.

That sense continued to grow as the conversations continued and became more concrete and action oriented. But there were two key sources of external validation that accelerated our confidence and took our project to the next levels.

The first kick-start was the catalytic interest and support from Ben Hecht at Living Cities, who saw enough potential in the effort to give us funding and staff support to begin sharing the Framework in other communities, to see whether our work could be taken to scale.

The ways in which we were undertaking this work clearly resonated: the emphasis on data and creating a base of evidence; scaling practices that get results; a communitywide focus on specific outcomes; engagement from a wide range of stakeholders; working with systems to drive change rather than working around them; and, above all, the power of committing to student success from cradle to career. Now, with Living Cities' support, we were poised to go national.

The second major turning point took place as we prepared for our first national convening in early 2011. John Kania and Mark Kramer of the Foundation Strategy Group (FSG) had profiled the StrivePartnership as part of their research on an emerging theory of high-impact, large-scale social change. This research was published in the *Stanford Social Innovation Review* in January 2011. The title of the piece was "Collective Impact"—the first time that concept had been articulated—and featured the work in Cincinnati/Northern Kentucky as its primary case study.

Kania and Kramer's research demonstrated that "successful collective impact initiatives typically have five conditions that together produce true alignment and lead to powerful results: a common agenda, shared measurement systems, mutually reinforcing activities, continuous communication, and backbone support organizations."[3] These conditions were clearly being put into practice on the ground with the StrivePartnership, and this high-profile recognition put our work on the map in a way that would ignite new levels of awareness and possibility.

When the article appeared, the phone started ringing off the hook with interest from education and civic leaders around the country who wanted more information about how to do this work in their communities. As a result, that first convening, held in Arlington, Virginia, suddenly had a larger scope, scale, and buzz than we thought possible at the time. By the end of that gathering, we had launched the National Cradle to Career Network.

Around the same time, Education Sector, an independent, nonprofit, nonpartisan think tank, had convened more than a dozen leaders from state departments of education, city school districts, youth and family service agencies, and other school and community organizations to explore the concept of shared accountability. The group of experts determined "four key elements for a robust system of shared accountability":

- An overarching vision of student success.

- Objectives, metrics, and performance targets aligned with the vision for each of the participating entities as well as for the collaborative as a whole.

- A system for collecting, analyzing, and communicating student-level outcomes data as well as information on the partners' organizational performance.

- Strong, sustained civic leadership, supported by an intermediary organization dedicated to making the community's vision a reality.

Education Sector then began searching for examples of communities where these elements had been put into practice and found only one that came close: the StrivePartnership of Cincinnati/Northern Kentucky.

"Although there are many examples of partnerships, networks, and other joint efforts, they are rarely organized to maximize their impact," Education Sector said in its 2011 report, "Striving for Student Success: A Model of Shared Accountability." Cincinnati's StrivePartnership is "distinctly different," they noted, "because it has a centralized infrastructure, a dedicated staff, and a structured process that leads to a common agenda, shared measurement, continuous communication, and mutually reinforcing activities among all participants."[4]

While there are similarities in the FSG and Education Sector characterization of cross-sector collaboratives, "collective impact" has eclipsed "shared accountability" as the term of art to describe the kind of process and framework that the StrivePartnership and StriveTogether represent. In 2011, collective impact was number two on the *Chronicle of Philanthropy's* list of top ten buzzwords.[5] And the White House Council for Community Solutions has recognized collective impact as an important framework for social change; indeed, the StrivePartnership was hailed in the council's 2012 Final Report on Community Solutions for Opportunity Youth as a model for community collaborative success.[6]

This viral spread of interest in applying collective impact theory to social change is a big reason we want to share this story in detail. Because the StriveTogether Framework was in many ways the basis for the theory, we feel a tremendous responsibility to describe how this work was conceived and how it has been living on the ground in several communities. While the broad interest in collective impact is cause for celebration, its buzzword status also poses a danger to the integrity and rigor of the work. There are very clear differences between this work and traditional collaboration.[7] But at present, we risk simply interchanging the terms and falling back to the status quo: working in silos and simply talking more with each other.

The only way that this framework can be taken to scale is if the people inspired to take on collective impact have a clear understanding of what is required and the tools to succeed. We want to make sure communities understand what it takes to get it right. First and foremost, success requires a long time frame and a commitment to stay the course. Second, this is very difficult and messy work. As anyone in Cincinnati and Northern Kentucky will tell you, the collective impact article is a sanitized version of reality. The struggle continues each and every day to align the entire community behind results despite major challenges. In short, this work takes patience and perseverance, founded in a deep commitment to real change in how we serve children.

As we describe in chapter 4, the excitement of rapid growth has to be tempered with a commitment to quality, and this balancing act is currently the top priority of the national StriveTogether organization. Fortunately, gathering lessons equally both from our successes and from our mistakes (i.e., failing forward) is part of the fabric of StriveTogether. The four pioneering sites whose stories are told in these pages provide value through both adversity and breakthroughs. In some cases, sites are still struggling. These lessons—along with the work of over 50 sites that are deeply committed to this work and helped to establish the Theory of Action—have become emerging standards of practice for collective impact. If we fully integrate these lessons, adapt future efforts accordingly, and establish a clear understanding of the defining characteristics of collective impact efforts, this work can truly be taken to scale.

At the 2013 StriveTogether convening in Dallas, the commitment to reporting out on lessons learned was on graphic display in a session called the "Failing Forward Fest." Having asked for a few volunteers to tell stories of where things went horribly wrong, we received 20 responses—for only three spots! One of the presenters, Bill Crim of Salt Lake City, when starting his talk, asked permission to tell *two* stories of "colossal failure." Why did so many people want to get up in front of their peers and talk about their missteps? We attribute this phenomenon to the culture of true collective impact work, where participating in this level of transparency is a badge of honor. There is a sense of safety in numbers and an understanding of contributing to real-time learning as a network.

In that spirit of transparency, this book represents an opportunity to provide a detailed roadmap to help navigate both success and failure and to support other collective impact efforts with the best practices and lessons learned from the StrivePartnership and the StriveTogether Network.

It also reflects our sense of urgency to address the growing crisis of unequal access to quality education in this country. As we work to reform our education system, it is absolutely critical that we pay special attention to improving the outcomes and attainment levels of the growing, widening base of Americans who live in poverty. The schools in our most economically impoverished neighborhoods need quality support systems the most and yet are least likely to have access to such resources. Right now, *every 26 seconds, a student drops out of school in the United States*. That's more than 6,800 students daily or *more than a million students every year*. But even with the shocking numbers—and maybe in part because they are so distressing—most communitywide efforts to improve outcomes do not start with the outcomes that need to move. Instead, they start with new programs and ideas.

StriveTogether's power lies in its ability to address this unsustainable state of affairs. By systematically improving local education outcomes, its framework can move the dial toward greater educational success and equity at the *community* level.

The cradle-to-career Framework that was born in the StrivePartnership of Cincinnati/Northern Kentucky is rooted in the understanding that we need to put the child at the center so that community resources are meeting individual needs. We have seen what using data to build on what works can do to improve test scores, high school graduation rates, college enrollment and retention rates, employment, health, and reduced community crime rates. Cradle-to-career partnerships are the dot-connectors that bring them all together so that communities can invest in what works for students.

So this book, while about education, is, somewhat ironically, not about children per se, because children are not the problem. Most kids, whether they do well or poorly in school or in life, are responding to the environments created by the adults in their lives. Blaming socially disadvantaged children and teenagers for their failures deflects responsibility from the adults in charge who actually can do something about it—not just a child's parents and teachers, those traditionally charged with overseeing education, but the larger network of adults in a community.

Likewise, teachers cannot be viewed as solely responsible for students' poor performance because in so many cases, and especially in poor schools and districts, teachers don't have the resources or training they need to be effective in overcoming the obstacles that accompany poverty.

So this is a book about and for adults who have a responsibility to create coordinated education and social service systems and who want to see these systems perform far better than they do today. It is for people who see the symbiotic link between strong schools and thriving communities, and it is also for those who don't need to see it, because the problems we are facing are their problems, too.

This book is for parents and nonparents. It is for teachers and non-teachers. It is for academics and nonacademics. It is for community leaders and business leaders who bring critical perspectives, expertise, and influence to the table. And it is for community foundations, philanthropists, and other government agencies that invest heavily in education solutions, with mixed results.

We share stories of how the StrivePartnership was formed and how it continues to evolve, grow, and help make meaningful, measurable impacts in the Cincinnati/Northern Kentucky region. Then we discuss the creation of the StriveTogether Framework and the launch of the StriveTogether National Network, as well as our evolving Theory of Action that is the foundation for quality in cradle-to-career collective impact work.

Next, we provide case studies of four pioneering communities that received "seed" funding to adopt the StriveTogether Framework in cradle-to-career initiatives, and the success and challenges they encountered in getting this work underway in their regions. Finally, we look at the lessons learned from these communities and discuss the next chapter of StriveTogether's work with member sites across the nation. With these examples and lessons learned, we hope to give other communities the inspiration and tools they need to undertake this transformational work.

We have been privileged to be a part of this groundbreaking framework from its inception and now are honored to chronicle the development and celebrate the success of the first national network of cradle-to-career partnerships. We look forward to continuing to participate in this extraordinary community of practice as it grows and learns together.

PART I

Origins and Organizational Development

CHAPTER 1

A Cincinnati Story

Cincinnati is the third-largest city in Ohio, after Columbus and Cleveland. Its greater metro area, which expands in all directions, including southward over the Ohio River and into nearby Northern Kentucky, is home to more than 2.1 million people.

First settled in 1788, the city's location at the confluence of the Ohio and Licking rivers proved auspicious. As a convenient outpost supporting westward expansion, the settlement quickly built itself into the first major inland city in the United States, earning the nickname "Queen of the West," or the Queen City, as it is still often called. By 1880, it was the most densely populated city in the country, and the fast growth spawned the establishment of other cities nearby. Just over the river to the south, Newport, Kentucky, was settled in 1791, and Covington, on the west bank of the Licking, was established in 1814, close neighbors to Cincinnati that today are folded into the greater metropolitan area.[1]

At the end of the 19th century, the region was a powerhouse of manufacturing and meatpacking and Cincinnati a boomtown churning with iron and cloth production and woodworking. There were also hospitals and opportunities for higher education, like the University of Cincinnati, which began as the Medical College of Ohio in 1819.[2] The region had much to recommend it and for decades drew immigrants by the tens of thousands.

But like the rest of the country, Cincinnati's economic drivers changed over time; manufacturing, once the backbone of American money making, suffered and all but went away by comparison to what it once was. Still, today the greater Cincinnati area is home to several of what can be called strong anchor institutions, organizations that because of their size and deep roots in the community are not likely to pick up and move away, big businesses that are big employers. It is headquarters to nine Fortune 500 companies—household-name powerhouses like Procter & Gamble, Kroger, and Macy's, to name a few. The greater region is also home to many colleges and universities, as well as nearly 40 hospitals and, of course, beloved professional sports teams, the Bengals and the Reds.

But as the 20th century came to a close, while Cincinnati had many strengths and assets, there were also warning signs of significant challenges.

The Greater Cincinnati area reflected the national pattern of struggling urban education systems. Nearly half of Cincinnati Public School students were dropping out before graduating from high school.[3] The numbers were equally concerning when it came to other indicators of the community's "education health": Kindergarten-readiness rates were below 50 percent, and reading and math scores, college enrollment, retention, and graduation rates were below state and national averages.[4] Too many Cincinnati-area students were leaving high school unprepared for the workforce or college, an untenable trajectory for the local economy and quality of life.

These results were alarming not just for parents, teachers, and school administrators but were enough to catch the attention of the broader community. Like many cities in the United States, there was already a multitude of programs and services in place to help at-risk students. But then why were the numbers slipping or stagnating at dangerously low levels? A handful of Cincinnati-area leaders found themselves asking this question in earnest.

Then, months before the events of 9/11 shook the nation to its core, Cincinnati experienced its own painful entrance to the 21st century, with three days of violent and destructive riots in April 2001 triggered by the killing of a young black man by police. Cincinnati, a city known as a good place to live and raise kids, was left embarrassed and stunned after the riots, Dan Horn of the *Cincinnati Enquirer* later wrote.[5] Not only was the city's outward image damaged; its sense of self was shaken. The riots of April 2001 forced Cincinnati and its neighbors to acknowledge that for all the good reasons to call the region home, there was a stew of deep-seated problems that were getting worse.

This combination of destructive events and frightening economic and educational indicators left the city with a sense of urgency, priming leaders to look for new ways of approaching problem solving, an open stance that may have opened the door just enough to allow for the embrace of a very different approach to education reform.

A New Kind of Collaboration

The work that ultimately evolved into the StrivePartnership was possible only through the participation of a wide range of leaders. There are many players, and many contributed their insights to this book. Chad Wick, then president and CEO of the KnowledgeWorks Foundation (KWF), had been thinking for some time about how to improve the systems that drive educational outcomes. At KWF, Chad had been involved with the creation of the Cincinnati Youth Collaborative in 1986–1987 and had been involved in local education issues for more than two decades. In that time, he recalled seeing many well-meaning interventions and projects fail to improve high school graduation rates, specifically. Try as they might, the graduation rate dial was virtually unchanged from the early 1990s to 2001. "My DNA is to look for system solutions," Chad said, "and the beauty of KnowledgeWorks was that it gave me an opportunity to patiently look into these kinds of solutions and invest in those that would further education and youth development in a systematic way."

Another key player was Kathy Merchant, president and CEO of the Greater Cincinnati Foundation (GCF). Kathy had long been tackling the city's quality of life and economic challenges with a group called Cincin- nati Community Action Now (CAN), but she and her colleagues had yet to make a connection to education. According to Kathy,

> CAN worked for nearly two years after the 2001 riots to identify a range of initiatives that would improve the lives and the prospect of a brighter future for everyone in our community, especially poor families and disenfranchised African Americans. . . . Those initiatives spanned early childhood education, getting jobs for "hard to hire" persons with criminal records and other barriers, affordable housing, better access to health care, and of course improving police/community relations.

When CAN completed its work in 2003, the group created Better Together Cincinnati, a collaboration of funders who pooled over $7 million to support development of several new initiatives that CAN's leaders felt were missing in the package of solutions, including the Community Police Partnering Center and Minority Business Accelerator.

By 2005, those new initiatives were up and running, achieving small gains to advance the community's big goals. But, Kathy said, this was still not enough. "While acknowledging that reversing decades of lost opportunity would take a long time, and that GCF had chosen areas of focus wisely and well, we still felt that we were missing an important lever for change."

Chad's and Kathy's paths had been crossing regularly for many years, and the two had become close colleagues and friends. They saw the necessary connections to be made between schools and communities. They shared a desire to help Cincinnati's schools and communities make those connections, and they had many brainstorming sessions over lunch or dinner about how their own organizations could work together to help more kids succeed in and out of school. They knew that greater collaboration would benefit children, their families, and their communities, but they struggled with just how to take action.

In 2001, Rob Reifsnyder came to Cincinnati as president of the local United Way chapter. Chad and Kathy brought Rob into their discussions because they felt strongly that they would need a partner focused on providing youth services. Chad and Kathy quickly piqued Rob's interest, but the pivotal role his organization would eventually play in the development of the StrivePartnership could not yet be seen clearly. "I remember having dinner about this with Chad and Kathy," Rob said. He continued,

> They had me asking, "What does the map look like for our education system?" There are a thousand players, but nobody knows who's doing what to whom and why and when. I was able to see that there were a lot of entrepreneurial efforts springing up here and there, and many of them were doing great work, but it was really hard to know what the big picture looked like. United Way wanted to be a good supporting partner in this work, but we really didn't know where we could fit effectively.

Upon reflection, the StrivePartnership probably could not have happened without Rob's leadership in launching the United Way's Community Impact Agenda in 2003. It marked a critical transition from the United Way and its partners simply handing out grants to assessing how grantees moved specific outcomes. There was significant resistance in the community to using data in this way, but Rob persevered and helped leaders embrace more data-informed work.

Then, in 2003, Nancy was appointed to the presidency of the University of Cincinnati and arrived committed to the critical role of a university to engage deeply with its community.

She saw that a university's active engagement in the community was essential to that community's success, to creating good jobs and preparing people for those jobs, to raising the overall standard of living and quality of life. She knew that for the University of Cincinnati to reach its full potential, it needed the benefits of a thriving urban community. She also knew that being the head of a university meant more than being a campus administrator; it meant being a bridge to the community, reaching out and saying, "This university could help make this city the best place to live in America by asking: What can we do together to make that happen?"

Building a sustainable and successful Cincinnati, Nancy believed, would require higher education to forge strong links with P–12. This was something that Chad, Kathy, and Rob hadn't considered as they had been focused on making P–12 that primary driver. Nancy understood where higher education was falling short in its service to P–12, and vice versa, and where both could do better together. To really see high school graduation and college enrollment and completion levels rise, it was colleges and universities, not P–12 schools, that needed to get smart and serious about improving teacher training and working more closely with school systems to see that students were on track to be prepared for college. This meant cultivating relationships and forming partnerships. And it meant starting new conversations, which is what started happening in Cincinnati in 2003 when these leaders came together.

Based on her experience as the leader of a large, public urban research university in Milwaukee, and leading a network of similar institutions nationally, Nancy was ready to see UC merge its agenda with Cincinnati's future. She knew that future would be defined by our ability to educate better: a better college experience, better-prepared teachers to serve in our city's schools, and a better success rate for graduating high school students who are college and career ready. In the very early weeks and months as UC's new president, her calendar began to fill with meetings with the key people on campus and in the broader community who could make this vision a reality.

Chad had met Nancy years earlier, when she was dean at the College of Education at Ohio State University. But it was her work in Milwaukee that had really gotten Chad's attention. He saw that her approach sparked a new kind of university-community engagement that had far-reaching effects in the city, including the performance of its public schools. When he heard that she'd gotten the UC job, he dispatched a letter to her immediately, inviting her to meet him when she got to town.

The two met shortly after Nancy's arrival in Cincinnati and began to build the table that would become the initial StrivePartnership. "We were essentially soul mates, connecting on several levels," Chad recalled of those early conversations. "We were trying to create an atmosphere around public education of finding the common ground among schools, universities, and communities. We were trying to get everyone on the same page, and as president of UC, Nancy seemed to be elevating everybody to a higher plane."

The fall of 2003 was an intense series of reach-outs, connection-making, and meetings, as their table gradually expanded and more and more community leaders joined them in asking, "What can we do together to improve education outcomes in Cincinnati schools?"

While the discussions between Chad, Nancy, and a growing number of community leaders were steadily confirming the need for increased collective action, discussions in key K–12 sectors were anything but galvanizing. Meetings with the then–Cincinnati Public Schools superintendent started on a positive note, but he left the position before any action resulted from those discussions. His successor, who had been a deputy superintendent in the system but not part of those early discussions with the Partnership, initially closed the door to further dialogue, a position backed by the school board, which had appointed her with its own agenda and set of priorities. Not without reason, these district officials were suspicious of "help" from the outside. Far too often, partners come saying they want to work with school districts, only to try to impose their will down the road. As a result, district leaders felt distracted at best—burned at worst—by community partners who rarely respected their expertise.

Complicating the matter, the head of the teachers' union was engaged in bitter negotiations with the board and had sent a clear message that there was no place for this new partnership at their table.

This initial resistance in Cincinnati prompted Nancy and Chad to expand their reach into the neighboring school districts and higher education catchment areas. The idea was that if they could get these surrounding systems to sign on, Cincinnati would be more open to getting involved. The strategy worked. Growing cross-sector support became evident, and the Cincinnati Public Schools began to realize that they stood to benefit from the effort.

Former Covington Public Schools superintendent Lynda Jackson recalled,

> Originally, we thought we should get involved with the Strive-Partnership because of money, and I think the district jumped on the train to follow the dollars. Then, as it evolved and things came to fruition, we realized it wasn't about the money. It was about thinking systematically about how we could build partnerships to improve student achievement in schools and work on the whole child, not just the academics, but also with community partners and parents and get everyone around the table.

Discussions with two area university presidents had quickly provided the added value Nancy and Chad needed. Father Michael Graham, president of nearby Xavier University, and Jim Votruba, president of Northern Kentucky University, located a short distance across the Ohio River, were also instrumental in the development of the Partnership. With the presidents of three major universities in the area vowing to develop a more coordinated approach to education from its earliest stages through college, P–12 support began to fall into place.

"We were concerned that too few students from our urban core were going on to college, and, if they did go on to college, too many were ill prepared to succeed," Jim recalled. He continued,

Each of us understood that college readiness required more than a focus on the junior and senior year in high school. A more comprehensive approach was required to align the in-school and out-of-school development of children and to focus on the entire education continuum from early childhood through high school and beyond. What began as a college readiness conversation quickly became a conversation focused on comprehensive urban education reform. I became involved in this initiative because I felt it provided the best opportunity to impact what I believe is the most important challenge confronting our nation. I continue to feel this way today.

Michael Graham echoed this sentiment:

Too often, we have tasked our schools to solve alone problems they are incapable of solving, problems whose origins in poverty and social change schools simply cannot solve alone. This kind of partnership enables a community to see how all of these issues exist on a continuum, understand what research tells us are the most effective levers for intervention at the crucial steps along the way, and muster integrated community support to enact change that works. As a priest, I grieve at the lost human lives our inaction creates. As a university president, I worry that not enough young people are adequately prepared for college. As a citizen, I fear that we are on the slippery slope of becoming a has-been, second-rate nation. Education is our future—individually and collectively—and this is a new way of addressing how we can get better results out of our educational systems.

This core group of top-level leaders from the region's three major universities, the school districts, and key social agencies and foundations later added the executives of several of the region's major employers and charitable foundations, leaders in early childhood education, and the directors of such civic groups as the Urban League. The Partnership ultimately became a broad and potent mix of leadership, skills, and influence, united by a broad common interest in improving education in the region.

The initial work consisted of significant outreach to the community as a whole. In addition to summarizing themes from years of engagement, community partners held a host of forums. In one gathering at Ninth Street Baptist Church in Covington, as one community member spoke highly of an after-school program she believed kept her child off the streets, another resident expressed anger and frustration that she was not aware of that program, that it was essentially left to chance as to whether her grandchild would be able to take advantage of the opportunity. And it became clear: With assets as precious as our children, we simply could not leave their future to chance.

Over the next four years, the conversation evolved, but the evolution was not always seamless or easy. We hope that the lessons learned in Cincinnati and Northern Kentucky, and the early experiences of other sites discussed here, can help other communities convene the necessary partners and seat them at the common table in a more timely and efficient manner.

A New Way of Doing Business

The community rallied around the concept that it was "program rich and system poor," but nobody had a clear path to determine what it meant to be "system rich." One thing was clear: Leaders from across sectors would need to work together, arm in arm, to develop a new way of doing business. Because this was not part of anyone's job description in particular, the Partnership would need, as Jim Votruba said, someone to wake up every day thinking about how to create this system by weaving together "what works" among the massive variety of programs and services in operation locally. It would take, the partners joked, something of a "cat-herder," someone with the problem-solving and task-management skills to bring together even the most complex set of professionals and programs.

KWF loaned Jeff to play this role and report directly to the community leaders at the partnership table and not to the KWF board. This decision gave Jeff increased credibility with the partners because it was their strategic direction he was tasked with carrying out, not KWF's or his own. Jeff listened to what the partners were interested in accomplishing together and formulated a strategy that kept them focused on their collective vision while meeting the "enlightened self-interests" of each partner. This way they could justify to their own boards why being involved in the Partnership contributed to their individual purpose.

The strengths and purposes of the different partners shaped the path of the work. Procter & Gamble helped lead a process to market the work. The districts were able to clarify what they really needed from the Partnership to help improve their bottom line: student achievement. And investors were able to identify the information and data they really needed to make more informed decisions. All of the partners embraced the concept of Robert Greenleaf's servant leadership without ever explicitly referencing it in the work:

> The servant-leader is servant first. It begins with the natural feeling that one wants to serve. Then conscious choice brings one to aspire to lead. The best test is: do those served grow as persons: do they, while being served, become healthier, wiser, freer, more autonomous, more likely themselves to become servants? And, what is the effect on the least privileged in society; will they benefit, or, at least, not be further deprived?[6]

With this approach to leadership as a foundation, the partners were willing to let KnowledgeWorks provide the staff to act as the "backbone," supporting a collective vision for the community as a whole. Their courage to lead in a new way made it possible for this work to come to life.

Articulating a Shared Cradle-to-Career Vision

The questions remained: Where do we start? Where should we begin to address the massive challenges confronting children in the region, especially those from poor families? What leadership roles might the various partners play to make sure the work is owned by the community, not a select few?

Given the critical mass of higher education leaders, the obvious first focus was college access and success, which fell squarely in the group's domain. Chad provided "backbone" staff at KWF to support the effort, under Jeff's supervision. Shortly thereafter, extended meetings were held at each of the three universities bringing together a diverse array of individuals committed to providing strategies and resources to make college access a reality for many more students, especially poor and minority youth support. At this stage, the effort was known as the College Access/Success Partnership (CAP).

By the summer of 2005, the CAP participants had formulated a vision and a mission for the Cincinnati/Northern Kentucky region; all students would have access to higher education and the opportunity to succeed in earning a degree. The education, philanthropic, civic, business, and non-profit sectors would provide necessary academic and financial support by strategically aligning programs and initiatives throughout the region that promote college access and success. CAP's mission embraced three primary goals. First, CAP staff would coordinate existing college access and success efforts throughout the region by mapping their efforts. Next, they would align those efforts with the needs of postsecondary institutions, school districts, schools, and students and their families. And finally, they would monitor their implementations and measure their results.

While improved college access and success had now been defined as CAP's ultimate goal, it became clear as Jeff and his staff delved deeper into student data and an evaluation of existing programs that the region was "program rich and system poor." There were numerous programs that were serving youth with the goal of increasing college access and success locally, but taken together, they were not moving the collective dial. One of the core problems was not a lack of *effort* but a lack of *coordination*.

It was also clear that the obstacles standing in the way of college access and success among kids locally began much, much earlier than high school. Conditions surrounding children's lives both in and out of school—often before they were even school age—were at the core of the problem. This realization had the group circling back to the concept of the leaky education pipeline and their earlier focus on a wider effort that spanned that pipeline from cradle to career.

"The conversation became, 'Well, what is keeping kids from going to college anyway?'" Chad explained. "First we thought the problem was in high school, but then we realized it was elementary schools, and then

"Education is our future—individually and collectively—and the StrivePartnership is a new way of addressing how we can get better results out of our educational systems."

—Michael J. Graham, SJ

finally, we said, 'this goes as far back as preschool.' And that is how it all began."

As their vision continued to take shape, partners began to pinpoint predictable and prevalent problems that confronted children at every stage of the pipeline and discussed interventions that could help children navigate those challenges and stay on the desired educational course. These discussions were the beginning of what later became the "Student Roadmap to Success," which was first sketched on a napkin at a local pub by a few key partners who were struggling to capture the new vision conveyed by their peers.

The roadmap was intended to be a visual depiction of the Partnership's ambitious goals for the region, serving students in school for the length of the pipeline but also providing more coordinated out-of-school supports beginning as early as a child's preschool years.

Nancy pulled together a UC team led by Larry Johnson, dean of the college of education and an outspoken advocate for youth, and his associate dean, Nelson Vincent, who worked with a cadre of talented doctoral students to develop the roadmap, a version of which StriveTogether still uses today. The roadmap went through several iterations before it was embraced by cross-sector leaders and began to be viewed as a guide for action late in 2005.

Asked to explain the importance of the roadmap, Chad said that one of its most valuable aspects is that the roadmap gives everyone involved in the process a complete mental picture of the work itself, beyond their individual scopes. "We come to this from so many different disciplines. We filter goals through our own mental processes, understandings, and emphasis," he explained. "The roadmap creates a mental model that causes everybody to suspend their view of the world and see the bigger picture. Because we all think in pictures, and the roadmap essentially gives us a picture of our interventions and what we are setting out to accomplish, it is a transformational tool."

Student Roadmap to Success

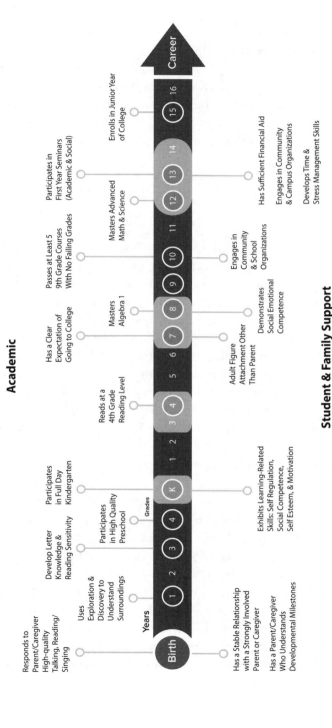

Academic

Responds to Parent/Caregiver High-quality Talking/ Reading/ Singing

Uses Exploration & Discovery to Understand Surroundings

Develop Letter Knowledge & Reading Sensitivity

Participates in High Quality Preschool

Participates in Full Day Kindergarten

Reads at a 4th Grade Reading Level

Has a Clear Expectation of Going to College

Masters Algebra 1

Passes at Least 5 9th Grade Courses With No Failing Grades

Masters Advanced Math & Science

Participates in First Year Seminars (Academic & Social)

Enrolls in Junior Year of College

Student & Family Support

Has a Stable Relationship with a Strongly Involved Parent or Caregiver

Has a Parent/Caregiver Who Understands Developmental Milestones

Exhibits Learning-Related Skills: Self Regulation, Social Competence, Self Esteem, & Motivation

Adult Figure Attachment Other Than Parent

Demonstrates Social Emotional Competence

Engages in Community & School Organizations

Has Sufficient Financial Aid

Engages in Community & Campus Organizations

Develops Time & Stress Management Skills

Birth

Years

Grades

Career

Going forward, we started every meeting with a display and reference to the roadmap, because of its compelling visual map of the journey from prenatal care and birth to career, and every important educational intervention along the way. It also kept the focus on academic assessments and improvement mechanisms (above the line) and critical social, family, and community supports (below the line) that ensure that children and youth arrive at school healthy, happy, and ready to learn.

The Way Forward: Launching the StrivePartnership

About three years into this dialogue, we got collective sign-on across Cincinnati and Northern Kentucky. The group's early focus on college access and success had provided an impetus for a broader vision, one that is depicted by the roadmap and underscored by the continuing leaks in the area's education pipeline. It was time for *collective action*—a more closely coordinated *system* of education in and out of school—that would serve every child, every step of the way, from cradle to college and into career.

The Partnership planned a public launch for the summer of 2006. We felt it was important that the start of our collective action commence in a symbolic manner that demonstrated both the boldness of our vision, which was shared and would be carried out by a broad cross-sector group of partners from both sides of the Ohio River, the likes of which the region had never seen.

Among the many bridges that span the Ohio River, only one is purple. Locally referred to as the "Purple People Bridge," its official name is the Newport Southbank Bridge. The bridge has long been closed to vehicle traffic but was repaired and reopened to pedestrian and bicycle traffic only in 2003. Rather than dividing the two states and four neighboring cities, the Purple People Bridge is a strong connector of the vibrant banks on both sides of the river. We felt it would be an ideal spot for our public launch. And so it was. On a sunny August 16, 2006, morning, hundreds of people from both sides of the river met in the middle of the bridge to finally and officially launch the StrivePartnership of Cincinnati/Northern Kentucky.

We knew we needed more than just the roadmap at the launch. Initially they planned to do a landscape analysis of all the resources available to children and youth along the cradle-to-career continuum. But Rob Reifsnyder had seen enough of these in his day that amounted to very little, and he warned the partners not to "asset map our way to nowhere." Based on the very challenging work the United Way had done to launch the Community Impact Agenda that marked a shift for simply funding programs to driving improved outcomes, he recommended we first agree on goals and measures. This would, he noted, give partners a concrete way to measure whether their collective work was actually having an impact.

In hindsight, this decision may have been what enabled the Partnership to stick. The primary focus on outcomes and their sustained improvement was what differentiated this work from previous efforts at collaboration. While those efforts centered on launching new programs or initiatives, this effort would be all about using local data to identify what is really working to improve the overarching outcomes. In all of this work, the

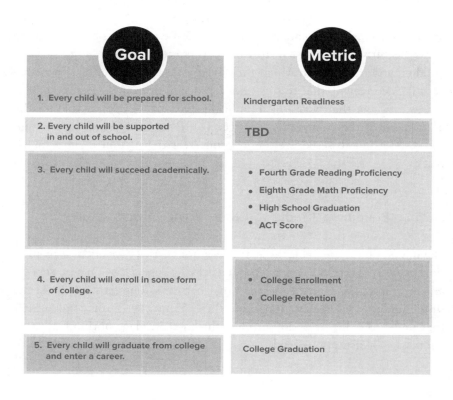

Goal	Metric
1. Every child will be prepared for school.	Kindergarten Readiness
2. Every child will be supported in and out of school.	TBD
3. Every child will succeed academically.	• Fourth Grade Reading Proficiency • Eighth Grade Math Proficiency • High School Graduation • ACT Score
4. Every child will enroll in some form of college.	• College Enrollment • College Retention
5. Every child will graduate from college and enter a career.	College Graduation

central question became: "How do we bring *what works* to scale to move the collective dials that had been stagnant for so long?" The data-driven approach to decision-making CAP embraced has since proved to be the only way to achieve a true collective impact.

In the end, the partners identified five major goals that the Partnership would collectively work to achieve and specific outcomes they would track annually to assess their progress.

Right up until the time of the launch, the Partnership had still been calling itself CAP, a title that marketing experts at Procter & Gamble felt was "too mundane" for the transformative signature effort taking place. In answer, UC's earlier development of the roadmap was expanded to include the larger task of branding, with the UC team ultimately naming and designing all of the materials used at the launch.

The community was rejuvenated by the launch. In an editorial published that day, the Cincinnati Enquirer observed, "This partnership looks like the real deal, and is making us an offer we dare not refuse." A new energy began to ripple through Cincinnati and Northern Kentucky as families, teachers, community leaders, businesses, and others began to view the StrivePartnership with high expectations for the future of their children and the cities in which they lived. The Partnership had been successful in conveying that this was not a program or even a set of programs. It was a system that would facilitate collective, data-driven action for the betterment of the community at large. The Partnership, and the communities it set out to serve, were now primed for that action to start taking place.

Building a Cradle-to-Career Civic Infrastructure

Having KWF at the table from the beginning as a "backbone organization" gave the StrivePartnership a critical leg up. This kind of support and infrastructure is critical to any partnership's long-term progress and sustainability. Unlike Cincinnati/Northern Kentucky, most communities that undertake this work do not have this asset in place until a concerted effort to establish one is made.

Pat Brown, a former KWF staff member who then went on to work with Nancy to bring similar initiatives to communities in New York State, spoke of the organization's role in making the effort possible and how its unique mission fosters ideas and innovation from within. "KnowledgeWorks is an operations innovation incubator," she said. "Their mission is to not only provide funding for social innovation but to get involved in the day-to-day operations of the initiatives they funded."

In Cincinnati, KWF's early commitment enabled the Partnership to reach the point of public launch with a backbone staff and fairly sizeable operational budget in place, and it afforded them time to spend focusing on other aspects of the Partnership such as the goals and outcomes. At the time of the launch, the Partnership also had some early in-kind support, with a loaned executive from Procter & Gamble and several point people from UC. There were early funding partners as well in the United Way, Greater Cincinnati Foundation, and Procter & Gamble. In retrospect, the only problem with this backbone support was that it dampened incentive for the Partnership to do any early fundraising, so its broader base of funding partners did not come until much later.

Likewise, it was not until years after the 2006 launch that the Partnership saw the need to define the building blocks, or the core characteristics, that were enabling their work to have an impact where other efforts locally and around the country had previously failed. The group began to refer to it as the process of *building a cradle-to-career civic infrastructure*. In the same way networks of roads and bridges join to create our nation's transportation infrastructure, a new *civic* infrastructure that connected the region's educational schooling and programs with the rest of the services locally that supported the growth of children and families and combined to shape their society's future was the *system* these cross-sector leaders had long been working toward.

The term "cradle-to-career civic infrastructure" is also meant to define the new kind of leadership we had embraced. Much of the Partnership's success toward having a collective impact was made possible by a collective notion of shared vulnerability and responsibility.

This began to define the collaborative process that had unfolded among them. Still, a more detailed framework was needed to support the momentum we were building, something concrete that could guide the process and keep us on track.

Fortunately, an important new partner would soon emerge and help us to achieve just that.

FAILING FORWARD LESSONS:
CINCINNATI

- **FOCUS ON OUTCOMES FROM THE BEGINNING.** Organize all work at all levels around these outcomes. They are the true north for all collective work and related decisions.

- **DON'T RUSH TO LAUNCH.** Let the results speak for themselves to generate a collective sense of progress and purpose.

- **FIND EARLY WINS.** Use local data to lift up practices that get results for kids.

- **SHARE OWNERSHIP FOR THE WORK.** Make sure the organization providing staff does not chair the partnership. This way it won't be viewed as an organizational initiative.

CHAPTER 2

Paving the Way for Quality Replication

A Framework for Cradle-to-Career
Civic Infrastructure

In the summer of 2007, Nancy was invited to participate in a working session convened by the Brookings Institution and hosted by the Rockefeller Foundation at its retreat site at Lake Como in Bellagio, Italy, that was attended by more than 40 key leaders of urban renewal. The session is where Nancy first met Ben Hecht, the incoming CEO of Living Cities, a collaborative of 22 corporate and foundation philanthropic entities focused on creating a higher standard of living for low-income urban residents. The two discussed the educational responsibilities shared between cities and universities, and Nancy piqued Ben's interest in the cradle-to-career work in Cincinnati.

After a series of follow-up meetings back on U.S. soil and continued conversations, Living Cities offered to support us to document/codify the activities into a concrete framework, to test whether this framework could be replicated in other communities.

With the support of Living Cities, we were able to have a KWF staff member, Pat Brown, observe the interactions, decisions, and activities as well as research the processes that had brought the Partnership to its current position, asking, "What are the key conditions that must be in place for this kind of partnership to succeed?" and "What are the criteria that each of those conditions must meet?"

Over time, this information was distilled into a tool called the Framework for Building Cradle-to-Career Civic Infrastructure. The Framework has evolved over time and has likely not yet reached its final form. However, the four *primary* building blocks, or "pillars," originally identified remain virtually unchanged.

Framework for Building
Cradle-to-Career Civic Infrastructure

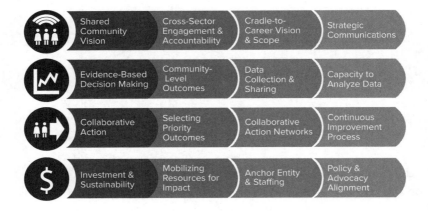

Pillar I: Shared Community Vision

A broad set of cross-sector community partners come together in an accountable way to implement a cradle-to-career vision for education and communicate that vision effectively.

Pillar II: Evidence-Based Decision Making

The integration of professional expertise and data to make decisions about how to prioritize a community's efforts to improve student outcomes.

Pillar III: Collaborative Action

The process by which networks of appropriate cross-sector practitioners use data to continually identify, adopt and scale practices that improve student outcomes.

Pillar IV: Investment and Sustainability

There is broad community ownership for building cradle-to-career civic infrastructure and resources are committed to sustain the work of the Partnership to improve student outcomes.

In the remainder of this chapter we will lay out the Framework in detail for each Pillar.

Pillar I: Shared Community Vision

A broad set of cross-sector community partners come together to implement a cradle-to-career vision for education and communicate that vision effectively:

- Cross-sector engagement and accountability: Representation from key sectors such as education, nonprofit, philanthropic, business, and civic and community leaders needed to develop and implement their cradle-to-career vision to which the partnership and community hold themselves accountable for achieving.

- Cradle-to-career vision and scope: A vision for improving education outcomes for students beginning at birth, continuing into and through secondary and postsecondary schooling until they secure a meaningful career.

- Strategic communications: The messaging and branding of the cradle-to-career partnership is to ensure a consistent understanding of the vision throughout the community. This includes using multiple methods to communicate the message appropriately to different audiences.

In Pillar I, partners agree to bring their collective resources to bear to ensure that children under their care and in their community can live healthier, more successful lives now and in the future. Cross-sector leaders have to hold each other *individually accountable* and *collectively responsible* for achieving better results for kids.

Central to the Framework is the integration of grassroots community leadership with top-level civic leaders (educators, business leaders, social agency heads, and key foundations) to form an accountability structure. It can be a struggle to adequately and consistently engage neighborhood groups, community activists, and family support initiatives. In the same vein, key civic and business leaders transition over time, causing partnerships to address personnel changes without losing momentum. But we have learned the importance of consistent engagement of top-level executives around a common vision across at least five sectors—education, business, civic, nonprofit, and philanthropic—along with ongoing grassroots engagement.

At first, this effort needs to focus on shaping the vision, mission, goals, and outcomes to which the partnership will hold itself accountable. Once a community has identified practices that actually achieve results for children, the community as a whole can mobilize to actively engage in implementing practices everyone knows will lead to improvements in what we call the "community-level outcomes." It is also essential that these leaders share a commitment to start breaking down the silos around these groups. The leaders have to be the ones to break down those walls.

As Kathy Merchant explained,

> A lot of people come to the table thinking, "What is this going to do for me that other attempts have not?" They've been through endless different iterations of strategy du jour. So every time we came to the table, and especially in the beginning, we said, "Trust is the foundation of this partnership." We made it clear that it was not about pointing fingers, and the group gradually became a "we." It takes a long time to sort that out, and there are no shortcuts.

Unfortunately, many efforts for collaboration with school districts start out on the right foot, with a community leader, college, or company genuinely hoping to work arm in arm with a school district to improve one or more student outcomes. As was noted previously, this second entity ends up telling the school district what it is doing wrong and what it should do differently. As one leader in Dallas noted when her organization started to launch a partnership, "Efforts like this often start by partners saying they want to work *with* the district, but very quickly devolve to trying to do things *to* the district." Because the children are under the district's care, the district is an easy target for criticism. Originally, in Cincinnati and Northern Kentucky, it was the general view of the districts that we were not seeking collaboration with them but rather imposing a directive on them as an outside party.

Partners in new cradle-to-career sites should be clear from the beginning that no one entity is going to be calling the shots; a commitment to collective impact must be upheld. Initial resistance to the StrivePartnership was gradually resolved as one powerful leader after another began taking ownership of the poor performance of students. Early on, at a meeting where more than 100 community leaders had convened, Nancy stood up and told the group that graduation rates at UC were not where they should be, not an acknowledgment a university president would generally make in such an open forum. She then asked for the support of everyone in the room in directly improving that outcome and promised to jointly develop data-driven action plans to help turn the tide. It was at this point that the superintendents and others within the K–12 districts began to accept a shared vulnerability *and* responsibility for addressing the challenges we all faced.

As a result of the openness that Nancy showed, people felt a sense of relief that sacred cows or "unmentionables" that had traditionally been viewed solely as institutional problems could now be owned as community problems, with an emphasis on "shared vision" to address them.

Cross-Sector Engagement and Accountability

Creating collective impact cannot happen, by definition, without the *collective*, that is, the people who together have the resources to create change. It is critical that everyone is at the table because he or she wants to be, not because it is required or because there is funding or prestige in it for him or her. It must be made clear to all individuals that data will be shared and will serve as the determining factors in any action plans that are developed, funded, and implemented. People need to understand the rules of the game *before* deciding if they want to sign on and are willing to work toward collective benefits.

In recent years, we developed a Value Exchange model representing the value that the executive-level partners and practitioners at the table bring

Cradle-to-Career Partnership
Leadership and Practitioner Value Exchange

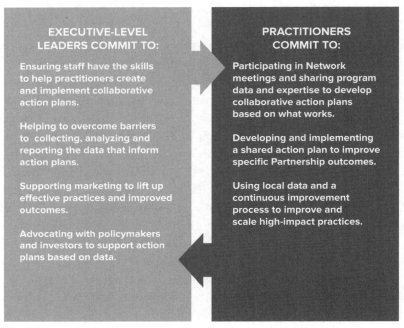

EXECUTIVE-LEVEL LEADERS COMMIT TO:

Ensuring staff have the skills to help practitioners create and implement collaborative action plans.

Helping to overcome barriers to collecting, analyzing and reporting the data that inform action plans.

Supporting marketing to lift up effective practices and improved outcomes.

Advocating with policymakers and investors to support action plans based on data.

PRACTITIONERS COMMIT TO:

Participating in Network meetings and sharing program data and expertise to develop collaborative action plans based on what works.

Developing and implementing a shared action plan to improve specific Partnership outcomes.

Using local data and a continuous improvement process to improve and scale high-impact practices.

to each other as a result of putting the structure in place. The awareness created by this model helps ensure that partners have shared expectations, and that they can meet their "enlightened self-interest," while appreciating the mutual exchange of value.

To create a sustainable civic infrastructure, leaders from throughout the community must come together to form a more *distributed* leadership and accountability structure where no one entity is getting either all of the glory or all of the criticism. There was a conscious intention to embody Harry S. Truman's notion that "[i]t is amazing what you can accomplish if you do not care who gets the credit." Shared accountability structure diagrams and definitions should be customized, based on the unique dynamics of the community, but here are some common elements of such structures:

- Top-level leadership committee: Cross-sector CEOs must commit personal and organizational resources to ensuring success of every child, every step of the way. Leadership committees typically define the way that they will work together through a few operational principles or guidelines rather than formal by-laws. Common topics addressed within the guidelines are meeting frequency and attendance; who, and under what circumstances, proxies for members may participate; and how decisions will be made.

- Steering committee: A cross-sector subgroup of the executive committee committed to meeting more frequently to develop recommendations for the full executive committee. This component of the governance structure was especially critical for initial organization and development of the StrivePartnership. Members of steering committees worked closely with staff to lay the groundwork for action to be taken during executive committee meetings, accelerating the progress of the partnership.

- Operational committees/teams: An additional level of cross-sector leadership is needed to assist in *implementing* the vision, mission, and goals of the partnership and serve as liaison between the executive committee and on-the-ground staff to implement the partnership's strategic priorities.

- Collaborative Action Networks: Groups of practitioners form around each individual outcome, working with backbone staff to look at their local data to identify practices that really get results and then build plans to utilize new and existing resources to take these practices to scale across all relevant partners in the community.

- Data team: Perhaps the most critical body in the broader accountability structure, the data team is made up of people within education systems who have data and experts in the community, including researchers, continuous-improvement experts from the business sector, and evaluators. This group helps ensure data are managed and utilized to inform decisions at every level from the leadership table to action networks.

Cradle-to-Career Vision and Scope

The first step in the process of creating a new partnership is *bringing the right people to the table*. Empowering those people with a common vision and uniting them in their commitment to effect change *from cradle to career* is key to success. Only when a broad set of community partners and leadership at every level agree to set aside their own agendas and work together toward a common vision is this work truly possible.

Partners take on a new vantage point, seeing the *education pipeline* in its entirety, as a continuum from the moment a child is born to the time he or she has completed a formal education and entered into a career. Each of the partners sees him- or herself as a contributor to children's lives every step of the way.

The formation of a cross-sector leadership table invariably raises a lot of questions about how each partner organization is currently contributing to the larger goals. Early educators prepare kids for kindergarten, but how much interaction do they have with kindergarten teachers to see if they are really getting students ready for what is next? Civic program providers keep kids active and off the streets, but what about the children who don't know these services exist?

Elementary schools help third and fourth graders pass standardized tests, but what more can they do to prepare them for high school coursework? High schools educate students in general studies and see them through graduation, but are those graduates going to need remedial education in college? Universities grant specialized training and degrees, but is a job waiting for someone with the skills needed to earn that degree? Employers create jobs, but how can they be sure there will be talented employees to fill them?

Asking these challenging questions is the first step to getting the answers that will start moving the dials.

Strategic Communications

It is not enough that the partners share the cradle-to-career vision. A significant part of the work is persuading the community. Establishing fluid and direct communication, both between those at the table and between the cradle to career partnership and the community it serves, is essential. Poor educational outcomes among children make for difficult conversations. Honest and ongoing discussions of both causes and solutions are bound to ruffle feathers.

In Cincinnati in 2006, the Haile U.S. Bank Foundation was formed by the estate of the late Carol Ann and Ralph V. Haile, Jr., who had wanted the foundation to fund strategies that aligned with their own passions: the arts, human services, community development, and education. As the Haile Foundation sought strategies locally, time and again they were pointed in the direction of the Partnership. They were intrigued by the work and wanted to fund it. However, they were among the first to observe that the Partnership was not communicating its work effectively. Truth be told, we had yet to really nail down a communications plan or even a general description of what the StrivePartnership was all about.

The foundation offered to take that task on and worked with a communications firm that identified a significant stumbling block in our communications: Partners had been talking about the process (how to get adults to work better together), but that message was missing the mark. Our purpose was simply to focus the region's limited resources on getting better outcomes for kids. More to the point, it was to "support the success of every child, every step of the way, from cradle to career." This tagline became our mantra and remains so today. The key insight was to stop focusing on the adults in this work and instead rally community members around children and their educational outcomes.

A separate communications challenge comes when you begin trying to spread the word outside of the education and business communities. Parents and families of students at every age have, sadly, grown accustomed to unproductive public meetings. Many communities are hampered by a lack of trust. This was certainly the case in Cincinnati and Northern Kentucky.

We held many community meetings in the beginning. You could almost hear those who attended thinking, "More of the same; all talk, no action." It took time, but as the Partnership started getting results by focusing on what works—as opposed to starting new stuff—and continued to communicate effectively with the community, they gained the public's trust. People began listening with interest, enthusiasm, and even optimism. And once we actually had data on interventions that work, people could get actively involved in something they knew would make a real difference.

Professional expertise and data are integrated to make decisions about prioritizing a community's efforts to improve student outcomes by developing:

- Community-level outcomes: Points along the cradle-to-career education continuum that are proven to be key levers that need to be moved in order to achieve the cradle-to-career vision and goals. Community-level outcomes are selected from across the cradle-to-career continuum and ensure accountability to the community.

- Data collection and sharing: The necessary processes, mechanisms, and relationships that need to be in place to effectively access and share necessary data to enable impact.

- Capacity to analyze data: The systems, processes, or individuals that enable the connection between programmatic data and student- and community-level outcomes to understand which practices get results.

Pillar II: Evidence-Based Decision Making

Pillar II, evidence-based decision making, is about *defining* the vision by choosing where you want to improve outcomes and building the comprehensive data systems needed to understand what strategies will have the desired outcomes.

Before work can be done to solve any problem, the partnership must first identify which "dials" it wants to move. Partnerships need to look at what the community wants to achieve and define, in very concrete terms, what outcomes will let everyone in the community know whether the partnership is headed in the right direction. Partners gather the data and let these identify the problems and dictate what they need to work on. Then comes the hard part: figuring out how to do better. The biggest challenge in this process isn't bringing all parties to the table, or getting them to agree that there is a need for reform, or even gathering the data. It's having the courage to *use* the data. Evidence-based decision making, shared accountability, and a strong commitment to continuous improvement through the use of data *to improve, not just prove* is what helps maximize results and capitalize on investments.

Community-Level Outcomes

The community-level outcomes and indicators are an all-inclusive list that encompasses what is most important to the community, whether it is improved fourth grade reading and math scores, more students attending college, or even lower rates of teen pregnancy. There is a tendency at this point to overshoot, to try and do too much all at once. Some communities want to start with as many as 100 or 150 outcomes that matter to them, but focus here is key. We encourage communities to narrow that list down to 8 to 10 outcomes that they believe are the most critical along the cradle-to-career continuum.

In Cincinnati and Northern Kentucky, partners initially went at this task all wrong. We convened a small group of top-level leaders and among us, without input from the community, decided what the outcomes would be. Naturally, when we brought them to the community and said, "These are what are most important and what we are all going to start measuring our progress against," the reaction was visceral. They were rejected because community voices were not represented in the outcomes selected. It prompted us to immediately take a step back.

Sample Criteria for Selecting Outcomes

- Population based, representing conditions at the community level
- Easily understandable to local stakeholders
- Reasonably similar across school districts/providers
- Data affordable to gather and report
- Data available consistently over time
- Useful in day to day work to improve student outcomes

We then convened a meeting with about 200 people in the community to discuss what the metrics should be. At the end of the meeting, the partnership was looking at more than 100 different outcomes. From there, the partnership asked for data analysts within the community—volunteers from the school districts and the universities—to establish a data team that would develop criteria for whittling the list down to a more manageable set of metrics. The data team took the first crack at vetting the list. It was later reviewed by the provider networks and partnership leaders.

Ultimately, the partnership was able to land on 10 community-level outcomes: kindergarten readiness and literacy; third grade reading and math; eighth grade reading and math; high school graduation rates; college readiness rates; and college entrance, retention, and completion rates. The list has to be this simple and comprised of measures that everyone can rally around.

The community report card

Once the metrics are agreed upon, we encourage all leaders, especially those with access to critical data such as school superintendents and departments of education, to agree to publish a regular report that will document progress or lack thereof. Leaders should develop criteria for selecting the outcomes and indicators that will be included in the reports.

As a first step in the reporting process, we recommend creating a baseline report around the community-level outcomes that also includes time-bound targets across the continuum. The baseline report provides a snapshot of current student achievement and critical benchmarks from which the partnership will measure its success. It is against these metrics that the partnership will hold itself accountable, and allow the public to hold it accountable, from this point forward.

Publication of the baseline report is also an ideal time for a public launch of the partnership, because the report serves as a catalyst for discussion within the community about the current state of education. This is a pivotal moment for all involved, where the partnership literally stands before the community, holds up the report, and says, "Here is how we—as educators, administrators, civic leaders, community groups, elected officials—have been performing on behalf of the community's children. We know we can do better, we will do better, and here's how."

Data Collection and Sharing

For many teachers, using data is viewed just as one more task to be added to their already full day. In answer to this challenge, partners have to make inputting data and using data as easy as possible, and we have to show users why it will make their day easier, not more difficult. In many school districts, for example, it's not uncommon for a teacher to spend an hour or longer at the end of the day on the phone with social service providers to ensure that their students are receiving the out-of-school supports they need to supplement their in-school education.

Imagine, then, if that same teacher could instead sit down at his or her computer and pull up a student's profile, add some input about the challenges the student is facing in class, and make recommendations for services that might help. Then the teacher could send that information directly to the needed provider in the social sector or, better yet, to a school resource coordinator tasked with ensuring that students get the out-of-school services their teachers recommend. This is a great example of the kind of high-impact change made possible by the collective impact work pioneered in Cincinnati/Northern Kentucky.

Capacity to Analyze Data

Once a partnership knows where it is and where it wants to go, it needs to develop a data system that will enable it to achieve its goals—a consistent and ongoing mechanism for sharing and analyzing student-level data across multiple systems to have a population-level impact.

The Cincinnati/Northern Kentucky partners knew early on that getting providers to regularly use a system like this would depend on how easy they could make it for data to be entered, analyzed, and translated into recommended actions. Critical, too, was that the data could be collected from disparate sources, with some handwritten, some pulled electronically from spreadsheets or grant applications, some from government Medicaid forms, and so on. Such a system would require money and time, both of which were in short supply.

We were fortunate, though, that just as we began to struggle with this, Microsoft approached Procter & Gamble wanting to do something productive in the Cincinnati region. As a key partner and one of Microsoft's largest clients, P&G immediately thought of our data dilemma. At their urging, Microsoft agreed to build an *aggregation* data system for us.

Another stroke of luck at the time was that the Cincinnati Public School District had just received the results of an audit that was done by the business community. One of the report's key findings was that the district needed to develop a "dashboard"—an easy-to-read user interface that provides a snapshot of performance indicators—to be more transparent with the community about how its schools were performing. In response, the district had recently developed a one-page dashboard for its website, giving Microsoft a head start on the data system, in full partnership with the district.

Microsoft and the Partnership then worked with the district and a diverse cadre of Community Learning Centers to develop the Student Success Dashboard.

Initially, the dashboard was developed only to integrate early childhood, K–12, and higher education data, but it has since evolved to include social service provider data and that of all children's services providers. Over the years, it has become a strikingly complex and inclusive tool. Program providers can now be very specific about whom they served, for how long, and how data are provided.

The existence of the dashboard—the massive data system that is being used by all providers, in and out of schools—has also created a natural overlap of children's services between the schools and the community. Before the dashboard, for example, local Community Learning Centers were focused only on making schools more neighborhood-friendly. Now used at more than 30 full-service community schools, the dashboard leverages the collective wisdom of site-level resource coordinators, teachers, district information services, student support teams, data coaches, and a wide variety of afterschool services, summer learning, tutoring, early childhood, mentoring, health, and college- and career-readiness fields. At the community level, Collaborative Action Networks from the same fields use the aggregated data to inform decisions around program activities, funding request priorities, and community engagement initiatives.

Key Dashboard Features

- Built around a school district and fully customizable to any community; school, partner, and data categories can be added.

- Enables integration of student-level demographic and academic data with services and support data from learning partners who serve students both in and out of school.

- Uses simple, flexible charting capability to provide the opportunity to analyze and better understand the overall impact of outside-of-school service providers on in-school student learning.

- Spotlights places where schools and community partners can invest resources to have the most impact on student success.

Since the dashboard was first developed it has been continuously improved and updated. The work is ongoing to incorporate more feedback from users to ensure that it makes their lives easier, as opposed to adding another task to their to-do list. Despite the complexities of this work, developers are finding ways to make sure multiple and diverse data systems can talk to one another.

Networks of appropriate cross-sector practitioners use data to continually identify, adopt, and scale practices that improve student outcomes through:

- Selecting priority outcomes: A subset of the community-level outcomes for focus, identified using local data and expertise.

- Collaborative Action Networks: Groups of appropriate cross-sector practitioners and individuals who organize around a community-level outcome and use a continuous improvement process to develop an action plan with strategies to improve that outcome.

• Continuous improvement process: The ongoing effort to use local data to improve efficiencies and effectiveness of processes and action.

Pillar III: Collaborative Action

Pillar III is where the rubber meets the road, where providers at the ground level begin to put the plans into action. In Collaborative Action, the providers who contribute to each outcome come together and build concrete action plans for how they will move the dial on that outcome. Plans are based on what data say will be best for kids and what will generate better results.

Instead of assuming they had all the answers and sending out "silver bullet" charges to providers, the original partners challenged providers throughout Cincinnati and Northern Kentucky to bring the community's "positive deviants" to their attention. This process identified which programs were already getting some good results, even if only a few students and families were taking advantage of them. These programs, the partners believed, might represent best practices to be replicated and scaled.

Selecting Priority Outcomes

The heavy lifting in Pillar III is unpacking the community-level outcomes determined earlier in the process and working on more specific, shorter-term "priority-level outcomes" that move the larger community-level dials.

Based on a review of the baseline data, existing successful programs, and stakeholder input, the partnership now determines its priority outcomes and strategies. These are a subset of the community level goals determined in Pillar II, reflecting what is most important and realistic for the partnership to focus on in the immediate term: "We can't get everything done all at once, so where should we start?"

Priority indicators and outcomes are determined based on where the community's most pressing needs lie. Common priorities include kindergarten readiness, early grade reading, high school graduation, and college preparation. The general process for choosing the priority outcomes mirrors that of the earlier selection of community-level outcomes. This time, however, the criteria are focused less on what the partnership wants to do eventually and more on what it can do right now.

Criteria to consider at this stage include:

- Is there an urgent need that cannot be ignored?

- Is there someone or a small group of people in the community who have the capacity to take this on and facilitate the development of a network to build a Collaborative Action Plan?

- Are the data available right now, and can we gain access without much opposition?

- Can we influence the funding around this outcome?

From there, a potential list is vetted through established committees, as was done with the larger, community-level outcomes, and a proposed final list is brought to the leadership table for its approval. It is critical at this stage—more so than earlier—that leadership at the highest level embraces the priority outcomes. Leadership must agree that if Collaborative Action

> "There are just times when you—in order to be part of something bigger than yourself or your own organization—have to either make some sacrifices or put some additional effort into the work to make sure that we are going to ultimately be able to achieve greater collective impact than we would if we were doing it on our own."
>
> —Rob Reifsnyder, president, United Way of Greater Cincinnati

Networks are established around these outcomes, and plans are developed to move these dials, it will support and advocate for them.

Collaborative Action Networks

Once the priority outcomes are identified, it is critical to form networks around each outcome. These networks are primarily made up of practitioners, but they should include other partners as well, such as potential investors, interested business leaders, and passionate community advocates. In many cases, such tables already exist related to a given outcome; in other cases, they will need to be formed. However the network comes into being, the practitioners need to bring their data to the table—data that show the good and the bad—and then determine which of the practices within systems and programs get real results. Based on these findings, the network develops a shared action plan for how to scale the practices across existing programs and providers in the community in order to advance student success in the priority areas.

One network that set the bar high for this approach in Cincinnati and Northern Kentucky was a group of tutoring and mentoring providers. About a dozen providers got together and compared results, and by working closely with the school district, they found that a specific practice was helping students catch up to their peers: A program that paired the same tutor with the same student every week for at least an hour was very successful as long as the student's teacher provided an up-to-date report on what the child needed to learn that day. So the group agreed to use a set of guidelines to replicate these practices across the schools with students who needed the most support. It agreed to maintain a consistency between students and tutors on a weekly basis, require those tutors to spend at least an hour with the students, and have teachers keep a folder of what students needed to work on week to week and share it directly with the students' tutors.

With these new guidelines in place, and the local providers in agreement to adhering to them, the partnership launched a massive campaign to place tutors in programs that used these guidelines, pairing those tutors with kids in the lowest-performing school districts. More than 900 tutors were recruited, leading to impressive results in some schools.

Continuous Improvement Process

Jim Bechtold, a P&G executive on loan to the StrivePartnership in 2006, really drove home the necessary commitment to data and demonstrated how a data-driven approach would propel continuous improvement over time. At a leadership council meeting, Jim pointed to a little black box he had placed on each table. He said the Partnership had been successful at bringing people together to talk about all of the challenges facing kids locally, but that they had yet to take it to the next level; they had failed to come up with any formative action plan that would address their problems. He invited everyone to open the black box, and inside was a piece of paper that said one word: *data.*

Jim effectively called the partners out for not embracing a data-driven approach. He introduced the idea that we needed to think about the work of the Partnership as systems engineering, proposing that we adopt the Six Sigma™ process improvement tools that GE Aviation—another local corporation—used to help make sure planes do not fall out of the sky.

Six Sigma is similar to the scientific method kids learn in fourth grade. It encourages all those working on a given problem to actually use data to better understand the real problem and then use the data to improve performance. GE Aviation agreed Six Sigma could be useful to our process and worked with us to adapt it for the social sector.

Datasets are just the raw material; it is the *analysis* by people on the ground that gets us moving in the right direction. So it's important that partners employ data analysts who can regularly sit with the providers and help them interpret the data to move program development in the right direction.

In 2006, United Way of Greater Cincinnati's group of early learning providers, Success By 6,® was preparing to release a report that showed appallingly low kindergarten literacy rates in the region but proposed no solutions. Informed by the ongoing process with the StrivePartnership, they instead shifted gears and hosted a meeting at the GE Aviation Learning Center with our partnership table, along with experts in early childhood programming and representatives from the school districts to look at data collected in preparation for the report and use it to figure out a way to move the dial on kindergarten literacy, among other measures. The Partnership was ready to put Jim Bechtold's theory into action, and he convened the necessary experts at GE to help.

We spent a full day at the center sorting through the data and training ourselves to digest them in what was, at that point, a largely unfamiliar way, all in an effort to determine what was really having an impact on kindergarten readiness. Toward the end of the day, after all of the Six Sigma experts in using data and applying continuous improvement principles had looked at everything, one GE analyst showed us how she was able to analyze the data to conclude that low-income children whose preschool classrooms included a certified teacher were almost always more literate and more prepared for kindergarten than similar peers in nonformal early learning environments.

We ran with it, and a couple of weeks later we pulled all of the partners together to figure out how they could attract more certified teachers to preschool classrooms. The University of Cincinnati found a way to increase the access to teacher certification. One of the big nonprofits in town, 4C for Children, made sure that preschool teachers going through training could get college credit. And the Partnership was able to acquire new state grants that would pay a portion of the teachers' tuition if they got certified and committed to staying and teaching in the region for a period of time after graduation.

In essence, the partners worked together on an action plan that engaged all the partners in spreading a practice—having certified teachers—that clearly contributed to improved kindergarten readiness rates. This was due to several partners like the school district providing data, the presence of analysts who could draw conclusions about what was impacting literacy rates and kindergarten readiness, and the willingness of additional partners to let the data shape their actions moving forward using the Six Sigma continuous improvement process. But the real key—and the sustaining factor to this day—has been the commitment of the United Way of Greater Cincinnati providing the basic infrastructure for developing action plans and advocating for what works. The current trendline: kindergarten literacy and readiness in the Cincinnati Public Schools has increased by 13 percentage points since 2005, despite major funding cuts in the state budget.

This work in early childhood provided the template for how to work with partners focused on different outcomes across the cradle to career continuum that we came to call Collaborative Action Networks. The action plans the Networks create provide a point of reference to look back to if engagement starts to wane, to train newcomers to the process, and to share with current funders as well as potential investors so that they are familiar with the process and able to track results. Above all, however, an action plan keeps the network focused and on task, working together to move an outcome using any and all data at their disposal that can help to inform their work.[1]

New partnerships are encouraged to develop a team charter early on in the process. Charters have four components: purpose statement, problem statement, scoping, and action plan.

The purpose statement is the network's answer to the question, "Why have we come together?" This is the broad, long-term focus of the group, such as increasing access to college or improving graduation rates.

The problem statement lists all of the factors that impact a partnership's purpose statement and the data available that contribute to those factors. In college access, this includes SAT and ACT scores, college enrollment figures, participation in early college programs, financial aid application data, and so on. This section of the charter should be as specific as possible. These factors and data points are the foundation of the network's focus in both the short and long term.

Scoping should be done annually to encompass what the network will try to accomplish over the course of that year. In scoping, networks generally disaggregate the data to determine where they can have the most impact. This could mean focusing on a specific geographic location, subpopulation, or any other way to slice the data. But it is critical that whatever the network takes on, it must represent a population that is large enough to leverage community-level outcome improvements. Serving 50 students may seem impactful, but this is too small a group to build the momentum needed to sustain an ambitious effort. Scoping relies on a constant review of the data and often involves a trial-and-error approach based on that regular review.

An *action plan* is also revisited on an annual basis. This is where the network gets very detailed about the specific actions it will take to move the dials selected during the scoping process. Action plans include strategies the network has decided to try in both the short and long term, assigning specific people to each task and to accomplishing that task in a specific time frame. The action plan also generally dictates meeting agendas when the providers convene.

Finally, *operating principles* must be established. When practitioners begin to share their programmatic data, there is inevitably concern that what is found regarding impact could be shared with the wrong people. The operating principles act as ground rules for how data will be used, as well as how the partners will work together over the long term.

There is broad community ownership for building cradle-to-career civic infrastructure, and resources are committed to sustain the work of the partnership to improve student outcomes by:

- Mobilizing resources for impact: Necessary stakeholders align and mobilize time, talent, and treasure toward improving overall community-level outcomes/indicators as well as the redirecting or initiation of resources (including knowledge, time, volunteers, skills, financial contributions, or other in-kind services) toward improving a common outcome.

- Anchor entity and staffing: The necessary supports to keep the partnership running operationally, including the organization or entity that commits to housing the partnership staff and ensuring its long-term stability, specifically through committing resources and convening partners.

- Policy and advocacy alignment: The alignment/realignment of policy priorities to move forward a collective advocacy agenda to change local, state, or national policy to improve community-level outcomes/indicators.

Developing and implementing a cradle-to-career partnership is a challenging task for any community. Gathering the right partners, earning each other's trust and commitment, putting in place a comprehensive data collection system, and adjusting to letting data drive the work; each of these aspects presents hurdles and challenges. Once these issues have been overcome, there is just one more layer to push through: ensuring that the partnership has staying power.

Pillar IV: Investment and Sustainability

Pillar IV begins with establishing a Partnership Sustainability Plan, which ensures that key partnership roles needed to implement the civic infrastructure are sustained over at least five years. Leaders may change, but their roles must remain intact.

Keeping the community engaged in the work over the long term can also prove challenging. Traditional tools such as regular town hall–style meetings and larger, more in-depth community summits serve important purposes; other, more creative means of communication can have a greater impact. In the case of the summit, for example, people felt heard and they did learn more about the work, but they did not leave feeling empowered to be a part of it.

Here again, the partnership tried to keep its tactics fresh by thinking outside the traditional box. We have had some success with recognition ceremonies, usually held in conjunction with the release of a new report card, to honor networks, organizations, and local community leaders whose work has had a measurable impact on one or more of the set outcomes. These events help spread appreciation within the community, not only for the efforts and actions of those honored, but also for the work in general. Such an event provides a platform for people to see that their peers, their schools' leaders, their neighbors—people just like them in many instances— are making a difference in children's lives. They can see that the effort is working and that people they know are responsible for its success. Instead of leaving only with more awareness of the work, they leave inspired to get involved.

The business community is especially challenging to engage over the long term. They tend to come at this work cautiously because it seems to be too time consuming, and past failed attempts have left them frustrated. Sean Parker was the head of Procter & Gamble's community relations unit while the StrivePartnership was getting off the ground. He said most businesses did not initially have the patience or long-term mentality needed to support the work, but they did come around once the Partnership was able to show them some short-term impacts of their investment and time, in addition to a promise for more over the long term. "Ultimately, it comes down to credit and whether or not you want to be a part of a large systemic change versus wanting to operate on your own and receive credit for something, even if it's smaller than what you would have been able to do collectively," Sean said.

Mobilizing Resources for Impact

Just as the Partnership held a ceremony to recognize people who had made a difference, it is critical at this stage that funders, both public and private, begin rewarding the Collaborative Action Networks that successfully effect change. This keeps the work moving forward and provides some assurance that there will be more successful outcomes over time. Funding for the Partnership is not effective when carried out with a "spray and pray mentality" in support of plans that may or may not be successful. Rather, resources should be allocated to programs that are generating better results for kids, as supported by the data.

The question of how a partnership will be funded for a sustained period of time must be addressed as early on as possible. These discussions, while uncomfortable, often difficult, and even premature during the initial stages, affirm the commitment of key partners and funders to stay engaged with the work for the long haul. There are three broad resource tactics to consider early on:

- Diversify funding streams: When a single funder bears the
  bulk of the operations costs, as was initially the case in

Cincinnati and Northern Kentucky, it can be perceived that the partnership is owned by that entity. Although we were fortunate that leaders kept coming to the table, there would have been greater overall buy-in and more of a sense of urgency if the overhead costs were shared by multiple partners (this has since become the case). This fact alone has increased the level of interest locally and secured a sense of accountability for results among partners. Cincinnati was able to avoid this fate because the CEO of KnowledgeWorks, the entity that put forward the operational resources, stated that (1) the CEO of the organization would never serve as the partnership chair, and (2) the staff would never report to the organization's board. Instead, other community leaders had to take on the leadership roles, and the staff would report to the partnership as a whole. This ensured there was broad and sustained ownership and that the process was not viewed as being owned by a single organization.

- Engage investors as advocates: As a convening body, the partnership can bring together funders who are passionate about their work with those still on the fence, expanding the roles of interested funders by pairing them with their peers, where they can share their reasons for signing on and positively influence those who are more skeptical because they "speak the same language."

- Identify in-kind support to attract additional resources: A key measure of a new partnership's success will be whether it succeeds in leveraging resources to achieve better outcomes. Identifying in-kind support for the partnership from the outset will ensure that these dollars can be leveraged to attract new resources, both public and private. At one point, the operational staff of the original partnership cost less than $500,000, but the in-kind support from partners quadrupled that, at more than $2.1 million.

Anchor Entity and Staffing

In addition to funding specific action plans that have specific results attached to them, there are also the partnership's costs of operation to consider. Critical to the success of any plan, of course, is that there is a person and organization behind it to see that it is carried out.

Early on, the Cincinnati/Northern Kentucky partnership had no real structure. Partners had talked about the work, identified goals, and even made some key decisions about how they would go about achieving them, but there was no central headquarters, no person or place that was tracking each of its many moving parts. We have since been able to identify the competencies needed for what is called the "chief cat-herder" or program director, in every community, as well as the data analysts and facilitators needed to make the work possible.

In the case of the backbone staff, the biggest hurdle is that it can feel like funding is being siphoned from programs to fund overhead. But if you consider that approximately $500,000 in staffing can influence nearly $1 billion in resources, the task becomes a bit easier. Having seen communities approach backbone funding in numerous ways, StriveTogether has boiled down some common options in a white paper entitled *Funding to Support Backbone Entity in Collective Impact Efforts* (see appendix A). As noted in the paper, there are key messages and a value proposition that show how investments in limited infrastructure can have a major impact on student outcomes.

It is critical to find funding for the backbone for a minimum of *three* years. A financial plan for this time frame shows that the partnership is here to stay. An established multiyear funding stream incentivizes sustained engagement by all involved.

The pace toward success of a partnership is dependent on the quality of the staff members who fulfill these core competencies. On the next four pages, we provide profiles of the four core staff positions that have emerged as necessary for a healthy backbone function in cradle-to-career partnerships.

Partnership Staff Profiles

 Partnership Director

Role: Provides leadership and management to ensure that the mission and core values of the partnership are put into practice.

Knowledge & Technical Skills: Knowledge and demonstrated success in organizational development; strategic planning; change management; project management; people management; financial management; educational policy and trends. Excellent written and oral communications skills and strong interpersonal skills required.

Competencies:

- **Leadership:** Oversees the work of the partnership by recruiting and engaging partners; facilitating the work of the partnership and its committees; providing advice and counsel to Executive Committee members in establishing policies and monitoring outcomes of the partnership.

- **Communication:** Establishes and maintains an effective system of communications throughout the partnership and the community to build and maintain a positive image; represents the partnership in its relationships with partners and the community; prepares key partnership spokespersons for speaking engagements.

- **Critical Thinking & Problem Solving:** Ability to address and overcome complex issues to achieve desired results.

- **Planning & Organizing:** Facilitates the partnership's strategic planning activities, including identification of vision, mission, goals, community level outcomes and priority strategies; organizes the partnership to efficiently and effectively achieve goals and implement its related activities.

- **Embracing Change:** Champions change and effectively manages the implementation of new ideas and new ways of conducting business.

- **Teamwork/Collaboration:** Reinforces collaborative approach in work with Partnership committees, staff, and other organizational partners. Supports and solicits input from team members at all levels to move the partnership's work forward and achieve its vision, mission and goals.

Partnership Staff Profiles

 Data Manager

Role: Supports the analysis, management, integration, and reporting of data for the partnership.

Knowledge & Technical Skills: Knowledge and demonstrated success in data collection, management and analysis; knowledge of education and community data resources; knowledge of research and evaluation.

Competencies:

- **Leadership:** Ability to work with key partners to develop a comprehensive community accountability system that incorporates data across the cradle to career education pipeline.

- **Communication:** Ability to report and share data with partners and community in formats that appeal to various stakeholders and audiences and facilitates evidence-based decision making and continuous improvement.

- **Critical Thinking & Problem Solving:** Ability to address and overcome complex issues to achieve desired results.

- **Planning & Organizing:** Plans for the collection, analysis, and reporting of data to measure the partnership's impact and to facilitate evidence-based decision making and continuous improvement.

- **Embracing Change:** Facilitates change through provision of timely and meaningful information and data for evidence-based decision making and continuous improvement.

- **Teamwork/Collaboration:** Develops and cultivates relationships with community stakeholders, including data and research professionals in education, business, faith, nonprofit, philanthropic, and civic sectors.

Partnership Staff Profiles

 Continuous Improvement Facilitator

Role: Supports and facilitates a continuous improvement process to develop and implement an action plan.

Knowledge & Technical Skills: Knowledge and demonstrated success in facilitating multidisciplinary or multi-organizational teams desired. Excellent project management and organizational skills; ability to create processes and systems, manage details and work independently; excellent written and oral communication skills and strong interpersonal skills required. Understanding of Continuous Improvement processes and data utilization.

Competencies:

- **Leadership:** Coaches, facilitates, and provides technical assistance to networks of community partners to maintain momentum, achieve objectives and complete deliverables, utilizing a Continuous Improvement process and tools.

- **Communication:** Maintains communication and works collaboratively with volunteers and/or data analysts to provide support for networks of community partners; ability to communicate with diverse groups and "translate" vocabulary/jargon across sectors.

- **Critical Thinking & Problem Solving:** Ability to address and overcome complex issues to achieve desired results.

- **Planning & Organizing:** Facilitates the planning activities of community partners aligned with the partnership's priority strategy project work; and assists in convening and organizing partners to develop evidence-based continuous improvement action plans.

- **Embracing Change:** Champions change and provides tools to assist community partners in accelerating the change management process necessary to implement and sustain their proposed improvements.

- **Teamwork/Collaboration:** Develops and cultivates relationships with community stakeholders, including leaders in education, business, faith, nonprofit, philanthropic, and civic sectors.

Partnership Staff Profiles

 Communications/Community Engagement Manager

Role: Supports the internal and external communications of the partnership and engagement of the broader community.

Knowledge & Technical Skills: Knowledge and demonstrated success in communicating to multiple audiences in a culturally competent manner. Excellent project management with experience in community engagement and relationship building.

Competencies:

- **Leadership:** Ability to engage a diverse set of partners from all sectors of the community and tailor messaging to their unique needs.

- **Communication:** Ability to communicate both horizontally and vertically within the community, tailoring messages so they are culturally and industry specific to the audience. Ability to identify target audiences and effectively communicate the partnership's key messages in the appropriate language.

- **Critical Thinking & Problem Solving:** Ability to address and overcome complex issues to effectively communicate the work of the partnership.

- **Planning & Organizing:** Facilitates the partnership's communications and engagement efforts to internal and external audiences. Must plan and coordinate a communications calendar to create a regular and consistent voice for the partnership.

- **Embracing Change:** Champions and communicates the change spurred by the partnership to regularly inform the community of progress. Facilitates the necessary shift in power from those with institutional authority to those impacted by the work of the community through the engagement and mobilization of community members.

Policy and Advocacy Alignment

For cradle-to-career partnerships to succeed long term, they need to cultivate a unified policy agenda that will align public and private resources behind what works. In some cases, initial advocacy may be for measures that help us understand what *does* work. For example, in Cincinnati, the United Way led a state-level effort to get a common measurement tool for early childhood education, leveraging partners across the community to wield stronger influence. Once the right measures are in place, the question is how you develop an influence strategy that gets investors to leverage existing resources (time, talent, and treasure) to support what actually works for kids. You aren't necessarily looking for new money, which seems like it might be an easy sell. But due to multiple factors, such as legacy funding and individual pet projects, it can be extremely difficult to steer existing dollars toward new efforts. But harnessing the "power of the partnership" can go a long way toward influencing changes to the status quo.

Our experience has been that in the early stages, it is best to work directly with private investors on an individual basis to identify which community-level outcomes they are most interested in improving. Twice we made a run at getting investors to agree to pooled investment. And twice, despite meticulous preparation, we failed. Eventually, we realized we were simply asking too much. As a relatively new and informal entity that had yet to establish credibility, we were not in a position to ask investors to relinquish control of their investments. So we loosened the reins. We engaged investors around the individual community-level outcomes they cared about the most and encouraged them to align their investments with those efforts. In recent years, StriveTogether has established enough trust and respect that investors are agreeing to some significant pooling of resources, but there remains a mutual understanding that their input will be a factor in financial allocations.

The same is true for elected officials and policymakers. They need early wins so that they can go back to their constituents and prove their worth. The Cincinnati/Northern Kentucky partners struggled to get sign-on from elected officials at first, because we failed to acknowledge this simple fact. That changed when we were finally able to secure some time with one key official. During the meeting, partners became frustrated that they were getting nowhere, and one of us asked, "What would it take to get you behind this work?" The answer: "Read about my education priorities and line up behind them."

The official's frankness caught us off guard, and the suggestion went against the Partnership's commitment to a data-driven—not politically driven—approach. Upon reflection, we realized we could line up behind certain policy items that were consistent with the mission of using limited resources more effectively by focusing on what works. But it would be hard to gain meaningful support from policymakers until we could give them data about practices that create better educational outcomes. Once we had this information, the policymakers would be in a position to align themselves with the Partnership's efforts on behalf of their constituents.

From that point on, the partners became more aware of the clear "policy wins" they could hold up for officials. The launch of a new, more comprehensive assessment tool for student progress, for example, can give a policymaker something tangible that he or she can point to, and align dollars behind, to support services a partnership knows will move the dial on its outcomes.

It's important to note that it is easier to influence policy over time, as trust builds among the different partners, and more data become available to more definitively identify practices and interventions that work. But even then, it is critical to develop a comprehensive and shared policy agenda with a clear engagement strategy that all partners can get behind. For example, when data in Cincinnati clearly showed that school nurses could be cor-related to improved literacy outcomes, the Partnership joined other com-munity stakeholders and successfully convinced the city to sustain funds for this role.

The format in which we convey winning strategies to funders and policymakers can be a deal-breaker as well. The key is to provide enough clarity without submerging them in paperwork and data, something that gives them the whole picture without getting too deep into the weeds. For this purpose, StriveTogether now develops a one-page concept paper for each strategy once a Collaborative Action Network has adopted an action plan. These papers outline very specifically how the action plan will be carried out, existing resources that will be leveraged, any new resources needed, and the overall impact the plan is anticipated to have over what time period. These papers keep funders and policymakers informed and set clear expectations.

Taking the Cradle-to-Career Framework to Scale

Once the Framework had been developed, Living Cities agreed that we had a solid foundation to build upon. They agreed to support the adaptation of the Framework in five other cities for $300,000 over three years, and to help leverage additional resources for each site selected in the competition.

This work was carried out in partnership with the Urban Serving Universities (USU), now affiliated with the Association of Public and Land-Grant Universities (APLU). USU is a network of university leaders whose public research institutions are located in metropolitan areas. The network name is meant to underscore its mission of outreach and engagement with the communities that surround its member universities.

The importance of these institutions came to be viewed as critical at a time where demographics suggest we are becoming an increasingly urban nation, with 8 in 10 Americans now living in cities and the top 100 metropolitan areas producing 75 percent of the gross domestic product, 78 percent of competitive patents, and accounting for 68 percent of the nation's jobs. Clearly, the fate of urban universities is increasingly dependent on the prosperity of cities, and vice versa. The role of the urban-serving university therefore is incredibly important to the viability of economic growth in cities at the same time that they face massive, cyclical problems of poverty, unemployment, and under-education. As urban cities face chronic teacher shortages, school budget shortfalls, and declining student achievement, the universities are called upon to provide increased remediation and heavy student support, all at a high cost.

This coalition of higher education leaders agreed to escalate urban university engagement to better the outcomes of both the universities and their home cities, focusing around the areas of P–20 education, building strong communities, improving the health of a diverse population, and fostering student achievement in college.

The presidents, provosts, and other university academic leaders in the USU institutions meet annually to establish and carryout a cross-institutional agenda designed to advance their communities. Nancy had been a part of USU since its inception and had served as its chair since 2005. This 40-campus consortium agreed to focus its work as a network in three "strands": education, health care, and economic development. The members had all agreed to create demonstration sites around these areas, and in the process seek federal and philanthropic support for their efforts.

In 2008, Living Cities teamed up with USU to issue a request for proposals for universities to establish cross-sector P–20 access and success partnerships, based upon the successful model in Cincinnati. Living Cities wanted to see if they could scale the Framework, using urban-serving universities as the backbones for these initiatives.

The Living Cities grant marked a distinct turning point. Backbone staff expanded their technical assistance roles with the support of the grant to the sites and their work remaining grounded in the four-pillar framework. The urban universities receiving support through the grant agreed to share lessons learned and help develop models for collaborative partnerships in other USU cities. They also agreed to be demonstration sites in what was at the time called the Education Partnership Implementation Network (EPIN).

The original four universities selected for the grant were Virginia Commonwealth University in Richmond, University of Houston, California State University at East Bay, and Indiana University/Purdue University in Indianapolis (IUPUI). IUPUI dropped out after one year, having been unable to meet the conditions of the grant. Soon after, Portland State University (Oregon) supported the Portland Schools Foundation (now All Hands Raised) in becoming a member of the network and took the fourth slot. CSU East Bay later transitioned their collective efforts toward a two-county STEM initiative. Finally, Marian Urquilla from Living Cities, who was aware of outstanding work by Mary Jean Ryan and the Community Center for Educational Results in Seattle, invited them to be the fifth demonstration site because of their own cradle-to-career orientation.

The sites featured later in this book—in Portland, Richmond, Seattle, and Houston—were the first cities to begin to adapt lessons from Cincinnati and Northern Kentucky captured in the Framework for Building Cradle-to-Career Civic Infrastructure and laid the foundation for the national Cradle to Career Network.

CHAPTER 3

Striving for Quality and Commitment

A Theory of Action

The journey toward establishing quality took a big leap forward on February 1, 2011. With the Framework under our belts, and a wave of interest generated by the *Stanford Social Innovation Review* collective impact article featuring the StrivePartnership's work, the original partners reconnected in Arlington, Virginia, joined by leaders from 20 additional cities who were anxious to learn about the work. U.S. Department of Education assistant deputy secretary Jim Shelton addressed the convening, commending the potential of our cradle-to-career framework to positively impact education outcomes for children nationally. "As communities and education leaders continue to work together to share and replicate their innovative ideas for comprehensive programs that work," Shelton said to the participants, "they will blaze the path to improving the education and lives of children and youth in distressed communities throughout our country." With Shelton's charge and the energy of the sites present, we launched the national Cradle to Career Network (now known as StriveTogether), with a total of 30 communities signed on as charter members.

Today, our collective impact efforts have attracted more than 100 communities across the country to use the Framework to guide their work. Since getting its start in Cincinnati/Northern Kentucky, this cradle-to-career, sustained improvement approach to education has been initiated or fostered in communities in 34 states and the District of Columbia.

As indicated on the map below, as of this writing, the StriveTogether Network now has 49 members. Interest has also been explored in Australia, Columbia, New Zealand, Puerto Rico, Malaysia, Canada, and the United Kingdom.

StriveTogether Network Members

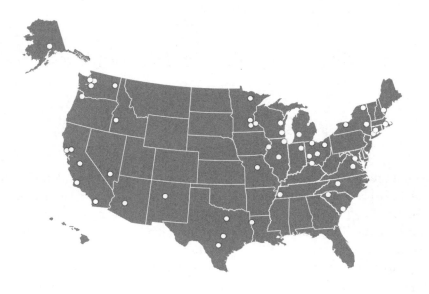

Forming a National Intermediary

After juggling both the local work in Cincinnati/Northern Kentucky and increasing demands from other communities, in 2011 the KnowledgeWorks board made the bold decision to fund a core group of staff to nurture this burgeoning movement. Jeff took on the role of managing director of the network, handing off the local work to Greg Landsman, the former director of the Governor's Office of Faith-Based and Community Initiatives in Ohio. Several other staff members who had been involved both locally and nationally joined Jeff in the national entity. This team worked in partnership with a core group of national advocates led by Nancy to establish a strategic plan in June 2011.

The plan outlined three key roles in which the national network would work to expedite the development of proof-point communities:

- Nurture the Cradle to Career Network: Ensure that sites are empowered to shape the field rather than thought leaders. As a result, sites are engaged to develop the critical tools and related resources based on practical experience. This includes forming work groups around critical issues sites are facing, such as establishing measures related to nonacademic outcomes and developing protocol for how to ensure disparities are addressed. In addition, sites are paired with peer communities and the national convening acts as an annual means to codify learning across network members.

• Provide strategic assistance: Based on lessons learned from communities, provide the best possible supports to sites so they are able to navigate emerging challenges as efficiently and effectively as possible. This includes problem solving in real time and constantly interacting on new and innovative tools that are being developed by peer communities. This work is heavily subsidized by investors, but to ensure local buy-in, a small fee is also required.

• Develop new and innovative tools: StriveTogether learns from common challenges that emerge across sites as they work to build sustainable civic infrastructure. Examples include the challenge of communicating the systemic nature of the work to diverse audiences, navigating the complexities of compre-hensive data management systems, and building the complex accountability structures that enable partners to work together consistently over time. We are working to develop user-friendly tools to help sites overcome these fundamental challenges.

A New Group of Champions

Along the way, a new set of national advocates who believed in the power of the work was emerging. This group came together in part organically, as significant national influencers simply reached out to StriveTogether asking how they could help: Sue Lehmann, a founding board member of Harlem Children's Zone and Teach for America who was seeking a way to scale reform beyond individual programs, became engaged. Lance Fors, the entrepreneurial board chair of Social Venture Partners, wanted to empower local donors with better information to make decisions and made a visit to Cincinnati. Others followed a similar path, including national entities that were leading significant networks of their own and receiving numerous requests for partners. Key leaders in the United Way Worldwide reached out to see how they could support their affiliates who were interested in the work. And investors looking to work at the national and state levels, such as the Annie E. Casey, Ford, and Robert Wood Johnson foundations began investing in the work to build the network and support individual sites.

These partners, along with some of the most experienced leaders in established sites nationally and the initial founders of the work in Cincinnati and Northern Kentucky, have come together as a powerful group of national allies. In September of 2012, these leaders were formalized into the StriveTogether National Advisory Board to bring the full impact of the group to support the network and achieve proof-point status. The board works closely with StriveTogether staff to develop the tools necessary to support the communities that have joined the network. Driven by the emerging needs of the network communities, the board agreed to focus on engaging national partners who can help develop this new national movement.

Steps toward a Theory of Action

The national Cradle to Career Network has the potential to transform the way communities take on complex social challenges. But it risks being undermined by one fundamental reality: Collective impact and building cradle-to-career civic infrastructure require clear standards of practice to be established and demonstrated at scale.

It was a combination of the efforts by the KnowledgeWorks board and the StriveTogether advisory board that fueled the rapid growth of the collective impact movement. But they were also the first to recognize that this growth could result in the concept getting watered down. Simultaneously, some of the most advanced sites across the country were becoming concerned that their work would be undermined by efforts that labeled themselves as collective impact but were really just traditional collaboration.

This combination of factors led the StriveTogether national intermediary to focus its efforts on developing an emerging set of standards for building cradle-to-career civic infrastructure.

So while we remain excited about the growing interest in StriveTogether's work, there is a concern that the nuances between "collaboration" and "collective impact" are not being made, that they are too often viewed as one and the same.[1] True collective impact work cannot exist in silos; however, in one community we observed nine simultaneous collective impact efforts on education. As we have shown, this runs counter to the concept. The more this happens, the more collective impact work risks becoming yet another education reform movement to fall by the wayside.[2]

To avoid this fate and to establish the development of cradle-to-career civic infrastructure as a standard operating procedure for the whole community, StriveTogether has worked over the last four years to establish quality benchmarks that will become standards of practice as we learn over time. We knew we needed to act quickly to document the collective lessons and create the tools needed to navigate the rapidly growing field of collective impact. But first, we had to create the infrastructure to effectively manage and harness the energy around the network.

As the network continued to grow, Jeff and his staff continued to focus on how to ensure quality. The four pillars discussed in chapter 2 provided an important foundation for the spread of the Framework to new communities. But are these definitions too high level to help bring a greater amount of rigor to the field? How do we help communities and partnerships dig deeper into each pillar while still respecting local context? To answer these questions, StriveTogether embarked on a journey to leverage the collective experience of its network of 49 communities.

The first step was to develop a Site Readiness Assessment to help identify strengths and challenges within communities and begin to identify common themes. This process started even before the national network was launched, during the first national convening. Using the Framework as a guide, the assessment helped communities identify where they were with respect to each of the four pillars. Then they inventoried existing assets that could be leveraged to get the work moving in their community.

To ensure that communities were using the tool effectively, those attending the national convenings and joining the national network were required to complete this assessment to help the StriveTogether team get a clear sense of current status and outstanding needs. As the assessments have been collected, we have been able to develop a common language and set of goals across all the sites interested working together.

Developing the Theory of Change

In 2011, a group of 65 sites that had completed the assessment met in Portland, Oregon, for the second convening of the network. National thought leaders spoke passionately about how they saw this work influencing the national landscape, and communities in attendance helped to refine a high-level Theory of Change. This was the first foray into defining how this work could unfold in a community over time.

This Theory of Change used the four pillars of the Framework that remained the core tenets of this work, outlining the basic steps a community might take over time. For the first time, the national network had articulated a general sequence to the work. It did not make the work prescriptive—there is no set of formulaic steps to take—but it did give a snapshot of how the work typically unfolds over time.

A Step Closer: The Progress Assessment Tool

Over the next year, we shared this visual with select sites that were really digging into the work. Local partnerships found it helpful, but there was a clear demand for something more detailed. While communities fully embraced the local context needed to shape the work, they also needed something that would help them better understand how it would all unfold. Based on this feedback, we developed the Progress Assessment Tool. For each component of the four pillars of the Framework, the tool identifies early, intermediary, and advanced stages of progress that sites could use internally, and with peers nationally, to assess their progress. A diagram of this tool is provided here for only the first pillar of the Framework, Shared Community Vision.

Theory of Change

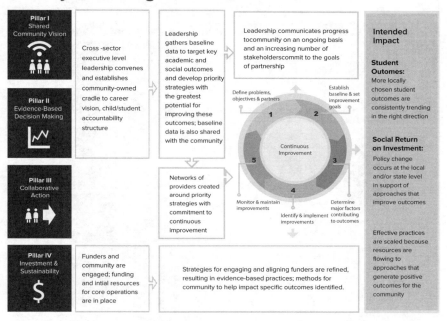

StriveTogether heard a great deal of positive feedback, especially when it reformatted the Site Readiness Assessment to align with this tool. But sites also voiced concern that it was lacking in several key aspects. The 2012 convening was held in Milwaukee, with more than 75 sites coming to the table. They brought more experience than ever, and the most productive sessions were when sites shared the concrete lessons and insights they had learned along the way. In summative statements about key themes from the gathering, it became clear that there are certain initial steps that need to be taken when building cradle-to-career civic infrastructure—regardless of local context—and we needed to establish a clearer common language and a foundation upon which the work of building cradle-to-career civic infrastructure depended.

Shared Community Vision

	Early	Mid	Advanced
Cross-Sector Stakeholder Engagement	Leaders from at least 3 key sectors agree on the importance of a cradle-to-career vision and to building the civic infrastructure to support that vision.	Leaders from at least 5 key sectors create a community-specific cradle-to-career roadmap and/or a vision, mission and goals for a cradle to career partnership	Stakeholders are engaged at all levels of the partnership including leadership, operations, and network groups.
Partnership Accountability Structure	Potential entity(ies) have been identified to lead/staff the development of the cradle-to-career partnership	An anchor entity has been chosen.	The anchor entity has incorporated its cradle-to-career role into its own strategic plan and communications.
	Partners loan staff or hire consultants to support the partnership (e.g. project manager).	A dedicated leader is hired to manage the partnership.	A dedicated leader is hired and all necessary supporting roles are in place.
	Leadership has started to identify the necessary groups or committees that would be necessary to support this work.	An accountability structure to sustain the work of the partnership over time is agreed upon.	An accountability structure is agreed upon with clearly defined roles and responsibilities.
Strategic Communications	Partners have a common understanding and can communicate a common message around the Partnership and the cradle-to-career vision.	Specific messages are developed to communicate the importance of the cradle-to-career vision to external audiences.	The community recognizes itself as critical to student success cradle to career, and is engaged in the Partnership.
	Internal communications between the leaders and the partners in the cradle-to-career Partnership ensures all partners are adequately informed in the work.	External communication channels are identified and employed to regularly inform the community of the partnership's progress.	Multi-level communication channels are established and regularly engage external and internal audiences.

Sample Progress Assessment Tool for Pillar I

About this same time, the Annie E. Casey Foundation and KnowledgeWorks invested together in a study to better understand how to best evaluate the impact of civic infrastructure. There were a few key findings, but the most important was that we simply had to define some concrete quality benchmarks to show what it takes at each stage, when partnerships first get started, when they become more advanced, and when they reach sustainability. These benchmarks would serve, after being tested for validity, as standards of practice over time for how to achieve collective impact.

Putting a Stake in the Ground: The Theory of Action

Based on insights from the field as well as the results of this study, we developed the Theory of Action (TOA), newly released in 2013. The TOA combines the best components from the Theory of Change and Progress Assessment Tool and adds new lessons that sites have uncovered as they have taken on new challenges. This tool now serves as the basis for how sites within the national network approach the work of StriveTogether.

The four underlying principles of the Theory of Action

Build a culture of continuous improvement. Data can be intimidating in any field, but this is especially true in education, where numbers are most often used as a hammer instead of a flashlight. To counter this pitfall, community leaders from Albany, New York, to Anchorage, Alaska, are creating a culture that embraces data to generate ongoing improvement. At the heart of this process lie the "Three I's": identify, interpret, and improve. Community leaders work with experts to *identify* programmatic or service data to collect at the right time from a variety of partners, not simply with individual organizations. They then *interpret* the data and generate user-friendly reports. Finally, they *improve* their efforts on the ground by training practitioners to adapt their work using the new information. Dallas's Commit! partnership provides a good example. There, leaders identified schools that had achieved notable improvement in third grade literacy despite long odds. Backbone staff worked with practitioners to identify the most promising schools and interpret data to identify the practices that led to improvements. District leaders are now working to spread those practices across the region, using data as a tool for continuous improvement.

Eliminate disparities. Communities nationwide recognize that aggregated data can mask real disparities. Disaggregating data to understand what services best meet the needs of all students enables communities to make informed decisions. For Portland's All Hands Raised Partnership, closing the opportunity gap is priority number one. They disaggregate data to make disparities visible to all and partner with leaders of color to lead the critical conversations necessary to address historic inequities. The partnership engaged district leaders to change policies and spread effective practices. Over the last three years, the graduation gap for students of color has closed from 14.3 percent to 9.5 percent. In several large high schools the gap has closed.

Leverage existing assets. The all-too-common affliction "project-itis" exerts a strong pull on the social sector, creating a powerful temptation to import a new program instead of understanding and improving the current system. At every level of collective impact work, practitioners have to devote time, talent, and treasure toward the most effective strategies. Making use of existing assets, but applying a new focus to them, is essential to demonstrating that collective impact work truly represents a new way of doing business, not just an excuse to add new overhead or create new programs. In Milwaukee and Toledo, for example, private businesses lend staff members with relevant expertise to help with data analytics so communities can identify existing practices that have an impact.

Engage local expertise and community voice. Effective data analysis provides a powerful tool for decision-making, but it represents only one vantage point. Local expertise and community voice add a layer of context that allows practitioners to better understand the data. Success comes when we engage partners who represent a broad cross-section of the community not only to shape the overall vision, but also to help practitioners use data to change the ways they serve children. In San Diego, the City Heights Partnership for Children actively engages parents in supporting their peers. Parents have helped design an early literacy toolkit based on local research and used it to help other families prepare children for kindergarten. As more families become involved, they are actively advocating early literacy as a priority for local schools.

It is critical that communities and partnerships in the Cradle to Career Network understand the science behind their work to ensure collective impact does not get watered down as collaboration. This is one of the key functions of the Theory of Action tool: to help establish the science and bring rigor to the field of collective impact. All network members also sign a StriveTogether commitment to quality, which ensures that they will use the TOA to frame their work over the next three years.

The Theory of Action provides a guide for communities that are implementing this work, and it validates what they are doing on the ground. It clearly lays out the steps the backbone organization needs to be thinking about to establish the cradle-to-career civic infrastructure and to make sure it can be sustained over the long period. With the collective experience of nearly 50 members, we have a solid understanding of what it takes to make this work happen. These quality benchmarks are a realistic snapshot of the critical milestones that new partnerships need to hit, related to each of the four pillars of the Framework. We have seen communities succeed and fail based on whether they crossed these hurdles.

The Theory of Action also points the way for how to take this work on consistently over time. The question remains as to whether all stakeholders—leaders at the national, state, and local levels, across all sectors, and at all levels from grassroots to grass tops—will have the discipline and patience to stick with this work to identify which of the Theory of Action's quality benchmarks are the standards of practice needed to move this work forward.

The Gateways of the Theory of Action

The quality benchmarks within the TOA are critical to ensuring a community can transform the way it serves children from cradle to career. Because the quality benchmarks are organized in a relatively sequential manner, the Theory of Action provides a clear outline of what building and sustaining a cradle-to-career partnership looks like in a concrete way. Sites are assessed on their overall progress along a continuum of "Gateways": exploring, emerging, sustaining, and systems change. Quality benchmarks align with the four pillars of the Framework within each gateway to give sites a clear picture of where they stand and where they need to focus attention going forward. By crossing through each Gateway, we believe there is a greater likelihood that communities will achieve population-level impact on students' educational outcomes and sustain this impact over time. The following four pages illustrate the TOA by Gateway.

EXPLORING

Partnerships in the **EXPLORING** gateway are working on the beginning pieces of formulating a partnership: convening the right people, committing to a common cradle-to-career vision for all kids, establishing the right tables to get the job done, selecting community-level outcomes to hold the partnership accountable, and ensuring sustainability through selecting an anchor entity to support the work.

A cross-sector partnership with a defined geographic scope organizes around a cradle-to-career vision.

A cross-sector leadership table is convened with a documented accountability structure.

The partnership formalizes a set of messages that are aligned and effectively communicated across partners and the community.

The partnership selects community-level outcomes to be held accountable for improving.

The partnership selects core indicators for the community-level outcomes.

The partnership commits to using continuous improvement to guide the work.

An anchor entity is established and capacity to support the daily management of the partnership is in place.

The partnership engages funders to support the operations and collaborative work of partners to improve outcomes

Partnerships in the **EMERGING** gateway are focused around accessing and collecting data and putting in place the supports necessary for data-driven decision making such as: an accountability structure to organize the work, prioritized outcomes and baseline data, releasing a baseline report, capacity for data analysis, a value exchange for Collaborative Action Networks, and the necessary financial and staff resources to support continuous improvement.

The partnership publicly releases a baseline report card to the community with disaggregated data.

The partnership collects and disaggregates baseline data by key subpopulations for core indicators.

The partnership prioritizes a subset of core indicators for initial focus.

Collaborative Action Networks are engaged and/or formed to improve community-level outcomes.

The partnership has in place the necessary capacity to support the daily management, data needs, facilitation, communication, and engagement of the community.

Partners support the operations work of the partnership.

SUSTAINING

Partnerships in the **SUSTAINING** gateway focus on using data in a continuous improvement process to identify improvements and interventions to impact an outcome, including: ensuring regular communication across the partnership, engagement of partners and practitioners to improve community-level outcomes, and mobilizing resources to remove financial, operational, and political barriers that inhibit the impact.

The partnership operates with roles and responsibilities as defined in the accountability structure.

The partnership consistently informs the community of progress, including the release of an annual report card.

The partnership communicates a common, consistent message across internal partners.

The partnership continually refines indicators to improve accuracy and validity.

The partnership enables the collection and connection of student-level academic and nonacademic data across the cradle-to-career pipeline and among partners to enable continuous improvement.

Collaborative Action Networks collectively take action to improve the community-level outcomes using continuous improvement.

Opportunities and barriers are identified by the networks and lifted up for partners to take action to improve community-level outcomes.

The partnership mobilizes the community to improve community-level outcomes.

Partners allocate and align resources to improve community-level outcomes.

The partnership develops a collective advocacy agenda to change local, state, or national policy to improve community-level outcomes.

SYSTEMS CHANGE

Partnerships in the **SYSTEMS CHANGE** gateway focus on navigating the necessary evolutions, transitions, and continuous improvement a partnership goes through to improve student outcomes including: evolving the structure through personnel and partner turnover, annual reports of progress and data to the community, the implementation of a comprehensive data system and continuous improvement process to facilitate on-going data use, and the alignment of resources around evidence based strategies.

Partners continue to actively engage in the Partnership despite changes in leadership.

Partners demonstrate shared accountability for improving community level outcomes.

Partners effectively communicate attribution of success and recognition of challenges.

The Partnership enables student-level academic and non-academic data to be shared appropriately across partners in a timely manner to enable continuous improvement to improve outcomes.

Partners use continuous improvement to identify activities/practices that are improving community level outcomes and spread these to increase access and impact.

Proof Point
Communities are in Systems Change and see indicators improving

Financial and community resources are aligned to what works to improve community level outcomes

The Partnership has sustainable funding for multiple years.

Necessary policies change to enable and sustain improvement.

PART II

Cradle-to-Career Case Studies

To get a picture of how the Framework was originally adapted in other communities, we dedicate the next four chapters to profiling the cradle-to-career partnerships in Portland, Richmond, Seattle, and Houston, describing the experiences, local process, and the challenges these collaboratives met along the way. These four partnerships—all recipients of Living Cities' catalytic funding—were pioneers. They have had success but have also made and shared their mistakes so that others can achieve their success more quickly.

The four sites featured were all launched in advance of emergence of the collective impact movement, so they did not benefit from the lessons and experiences of others. In fact, some of the choices made by these communities have required significant effort to right the ship, maintain momentum, and gain meaningful traction. But as a result, cradle-to-career communities coming on line today benefit directly from the contributions of these trailblazers.

Since the launch of the StriveTogether network, we have been documenting the progress of sites through a longitudinal evaluation process of the long-term impact of the cradle-to-career civic infrastructure on outcomes. We'll continue to report on that study in the future as our community of practice learns and grows in real time.

We are indeed fortunate that the leaders of the communities featured in the next four chapters have been so gracious in exemplifying the ethic of failing forward—an approach that has laid a solid foundation as this very challenging yet highly effective framework is brought to scale.

CHAPTER 4

Portland

All Hands Raised

Not unlike the many communities nationally that have adopted the StriveTogether Framework, the 2011 educational statistics for Portland, Oregon, and the surrounding Multnomah County were sobering. Portland Public Schools was (and is) the largest public school district in Oregon, serving over 47,000 students in 81 schools. More than 35 percent of all students did not graduate from high school, and the on-time graduation rate for Portland Public Schools that year was an anemic 62 percent. Further, only 33 percent of ninth graders in Oregon who finished high school went on to attend college, and almost 40 percent of students in Multnomah County did not earn a diploma on time. For students of color, the numbers were even more devastating, with the achievement gap entrenched at all stages. The four-year graduation rates for African Americans dropped to 46 percent and for Latinos dropped to 34 percent. Students of color were accessing college at significantly lower rates than their white counterparts, and those who did enroll were less likely to graduate. And this is just for one of the six districts in Multnomah County; the data were equally startling for the smaller districts serving students in Portland.

The economic consequences of these numbers were, and still are, equally devastating for students and their families, as well as the larger Portland community. Thirteen percent of families and nearly one-fifth of all Portland residents were below the federal poverty level in 2011. More than one-fifth of families with children and almost a quarter of all children under 18 were also below the poverty level. And almost half of all families headed by single females with children were below the poverty level.

The Lay of the Land

In 2010, the Portland Business Alliance along with the Associated Oregon Industries, the Oregon Business Council, the Port of Portland, and the Oregon Business Association, commissioned a study titled "A Check-Up on the Portland Region's Economic Health"[1] in answer to the growing economic crisis in the region. Where previously Portland had enjoyed relative economic health, its economic performance was not keeping pace with a number of its peer cities around the nation. The region's per-capita income lagged anywhere from 16 to 21 percent behind those of Seattle, Denver, and Minneapolis, and more than 26,000 private-sector jobs left the area between 1997 and 2009. Growth was stagnant, with Multnomah County ranking 198th out of 199 in private-sector job creation in the five western states from 1999 to 2009.

With lower wages and incomes than residents of peer regions, Portland was suffering from severe budget shortages for education, law enforcement, social services, and other important public services. Between 2009 and 2011 alone, the Portland Public Schools (PPS) budget was cut by over $28 million. The report calculated that if Metro Portland's per-capita income equaled Metro Seattle's, there would be $23.4 billion more in personal income and an additional $86.6 million in school support.

The report showed that the Metro Portland region was facing a true crisis: significant job loss, declining wages, and severe underinvestment in the region's schools, universities, parks, ports, and human services.

In the mid-1990s, in the wake of significant cuts to public education, the Portland Schools Foundation (PSF) was established to steward PPS parent-led fundraising. It was charged with managing the redistribution of a portion of those funds to the highest-need schools through the PPS Equity Fund in an effort to ensure equity across the district. Through this work the organization became a beacon in the community for ensuring an equitable education for all kids regardless of their race, zip code, or economic circumstances.

The organization expanded its work beyond this traditional scope in 2007 when it conducted groundbreaking research and published findings showing that the graduation rates of local high schools was far lower than previously documented.

The publication of this research, *Connected by 25*, galvanized community groups, schools, business leaders, and policymakers around the vision that all Portland youth should be better connected with school, work, and the community by the age of 25.[2] *Connected by 25* illuminated a number of issues and strategies that needed action, including identifying the key indicators of eighth graders' likelihood to be on track to graduate from high school. As a result, the summer between eighth and ninth grade was identified as a significant point of intervention for those students identified as at risk of dropping out or of "academic priority."

As a result of this information, the PSF brought together a diverse set of partners (including its historical partner PPS and five other local urban districts in Multnomah County) committed to addressing this crucial transition point in the educational pipeline. The first full roster of coordinated programs was rolled out as Ninth Grade Counts to eighth graders, their counselors, parents, and teachers for the summer of 2009. The establishment of Ninth Grade Counts was also important in that it brought together the school districts in Multnomah County around a key point in the education continuum and engaged culturally specific organizations in a meaningful way. Subsequently, the six superintendents adopted a common definition for an "academic priority" student—those at risk of dropping out—and began a shared flagging system in their databases to track these students and their progress. With the launch of *Connected by 25* and Ninth Grade Counts, Portland leaders were already showing an interest and orientation toward a cradle-to-career approach.

In 2008, Portland city commissioner Sam Adams was running his election campaign for mayor on an education platform, using the *Connected by 25* data as a canary in the coalmine for Portland. Adams made the connection between a more educated workforce and economic prosperity for the region and won the election in a landslide with 59 percent of the vote and a record turnout exceeding 60 percent of voters. Upon his election, Adams and then Multnomah County chair Ted Wheeler placed high school graduation and college access at the top of their agendas forming a co-led education cabinet in hopes of establishing greater alignment in the county around a broad set of student success strategies, especially focused on high school completion.

By the summer of 2009, at a time of record national youth unemployment, federal stimulus dollars helped hundreds of local employers put more than 800 low-income youth to work across Multnomah County. The mayor's office led a related initiative in which dozens of businesses and colleges hosted site visits and provided job shadowing for more than 400 at-risk incoming ninth graders. Finally, the Multnomah Youth Commission, a diverse group of youth leaders, won support for a program to provide free access to public transportation for 13,000 PPS high school students as part of an effort to better coordinate between school, work, and the community. Things seemed to be moving in the right direction as members of the community began collaborating around the mayor's Future Connect initiative aimed at improving the lives of students in the greater Portland area.

This work galvanized leaders from the community, especially leaders from communities of color who had been voicing their frustration for decades. Joyce Harris was director of Education Northwest's Equity Center, a center that worked through the U.S. Department of Education on issues related to race, gender, and national origin equity. Harris served on the mayor's education cabinet and was happy with the progress being made when Ninth Grade Counts was introduced, personally training all the volunteers in cultural competency before they met with and helped the youth being targeted. Having been in the Metro Portland area for some time, she knew just how bad the situation had become. "I happen to be someone who is very involved in the community and I can't begin to tell you how many funerals of young people I have gone to this year. Two fourteen-year-olds; I mean needless, senseless violence. I've told everyone this—that we are either going to sink or swim together," she recalled.

A Higher Ed Partner

In May 2008, Portland State University (PSU) announced its selection of Wim Wiewel as its new president. PSU has a sterling reputation in the Metro Portland area as an institution of higher education deeply committed to community engagement and sustainability. With a background in urban and public affairs, Wim was a natural fit for the position and hit the ground running in fall of 2008, meeting with each department head to figure out how PSU could better serve the surrounding community.

When the new president met with Randy Hitz, the dean of education, Wim laid down his vision for PSU's commitment to the education community in Portland. "I came in and told Randy, 'we've got to get organized. We need to do much more with K–12 than we are. Maybe you're doing a million things, but it sure doesn't show up on our website, and what are we going to do about it?'"

Randy had heard about the cradle-to-career work being done in Cincinnati, had visited the site, and pitched the concept to Wim, who was working with both the leaders roundtable and the education cabinet. Wim realized that the two groups were working on affecting the same outcome but weren't working together. He decided to bring up this glaring problem at the June meeting in 2009 of the leaders' roundtable:

> We were at their retreat at the end of my first year, right after we had gotten the start-up money from Living Cities . . . I really made a plea that we should embrace this as an absolute major focus of the whole education establishment in the region with all the superintendents and that PSU was prepared to make a significant investment. We had done just that by hiring a data manager who was going to collect the data to do a progress report, and people were really energized by that.

At the next meeting of the leaders' roundtable in September 2009, the group who had studied Cincinnati's framework presented the idea to the body, including the mayor who had been absent from the summer meeting. Mayor Adams was initially concerned about duplicating the efforts that had already been underway but saw the possibility in creating a larger vision for the work that encompassed birth to career. He remembered:

> I think it took maybe a month before we actually had the chance to sit down with him to basically say, "Listen, your initiative is one very important piece of this larger pipeline, but it is a pipeline . . . You can't be the only one who owns it because whenever a mayor solely owns this kind of initiative, a lot of other people see it as electoral politics. They're not really going

to be interested or motivated. You've got to be willing to see how your part is simply one part of the larger whole."

Calling a seamless pipeline from birth to career "radical common sense," the mayor realized the only way for the work to make progress was to reshape how the community was coming together to address educational outcomes. Given that the leaders' roundtable and the education cabinet were made up roughly 80 percent by the same people, Adams offered to abolish the education cabinet if the leaders' roundtable also folded in favor of a new, wide-spanning, cradle-to-career table.

As a result of this new, shared vision, a creation committee was established in the spring of 2010 and a request for proposals was released to the community to identify an organization to lead this effort.

In July 2008, Dan Ryan was selected to take over as the third CEO of the PSF. With over 25 years of nonprofit management experience, including being chair of the PPS board at the time of his hire, he was uniquely positioned to lead the organization into an era of growth. Dan recalled:

> It was time to rethink what this organization could do with its mission, which is really about ensuring a quality education for every kid in every neighborhood and really focusing on equity. But we were stuck on how to implement this mission. "How we could be useful? How can we effectively leverage outcomes for all? How can we be an intermediary between the schools and the business community, the schools and the nonprofits? How can we convene in a way that truly breaks down the silos and aligns and expands learning and supports outside of the bell schedule?" . . . So for me, when the cradle-to-career opportunity came to this market through Portland State University, I knew within ten seconds that we were the organization that was supposed to lead this.

In the summer of 2010 the PSF submitted its application to the creation committee to become the entity that would manage the local cradle-to-career work in Multnomah County. At the urging of the six superintendents and countless nonprofit organizations, PSF was selected.

On November 30, in a middle school library packed with more than 100 leaders, the education cabinet and the leaders' roundtable voted to dissolve their own organizations and empower the PSF to lead the new community-wide cradle-to-career effort. This was a major turning point for the partnership and a great example of existing structures willingly closing shop to move into a new blended alliance around a shared vision.

Critical to the selection of PSF as the lead entity were the solid and diverse board of directors and the team of staff that Dan had built since taking over as CEO. This included a chief financial officer capable of handling a multi-million-dollar nonprofit budget; a knowledgeable, a well-respected community engagement professional; a top-notch communicator to frame the story and keep the community abreast of progress; a seasoned development professional; and a team coordinator capable of keeping everyone on time, on schedule, and on mission. Couple that with a culturally diverse board, and the organization was primed for this community leadership role.

The PSF board of directors charged a taskforce, led by board member and then Qwest CEO Judy Peppler (now president and CEO of KnowledgeWorks), with representation from a cross-section of leaders, with developing the mission and responsibilities of an advisory-level council for the partnership. They developed criteria for inclusive representation of the community and a tentative roster of individuals to be invited to serve on it. The council, co-chaired by Judy and NW Natural CEO Gregg Kantor and comprised of 43 CEO-level cross-sector executives, met for the first time in the spring of 2011, launching the work on behalf of the greater community.

At the same time, two subcommittees of the PSF board were established (the steering committee and the data team) and charged with advising both this new council and the board with ensuring the regular collection, synthesis, and reporting of data to track progress on major indicators and guide the development of strategic priorities.

At the time PSF became the backbone organization for the work, and at the urging of the six superintendents, the organization was advised to map out a name change that would both signal an expanded purpose to the greater community and affirm its historical roots. Due to the organization's history, it was clear that the process to engage the community in the work and in the rebranding was as important as the eventual outcome of the process. In October of 2011, PSF rebranded itself as All Hands Raised, a name that underscored shared accountability and collective impact. Equally important was the creation of the tagline "Education, Equity and Excellence from Cradle to Career." The partnership was well on its way to changing the civic infrastructure of greater Portland.

Gaining Focus, Getting Started

One of the very first actions taken up by the new council was establishing priorities to guide the work. In an initial brainstorming session, the steering committee generated an overwhelming list of different priorities that could provide roots for future work. Both council co-chairs and Dan Ryan advised the steering committee that the goal was to narrow the scope of priorities to three. Dan recalled:

> It was not easy to get to three, and the process said a lot . . . We started with the steering committee putting 27 priorities up. In my role, I had to stay in a very clear lane that we only had the capacity to manage three. And I was very clear that we—as a community—could only manage expectations of three. Oftentimes, when there is a big idea and a lot of stakeholders, we want to please everyone by letting them have their priority listed, but then you leave with double-digit priorities, and then a year later you're left with a lot of frustration because nothing really happened because you didn't have the capacity.

After considerable discussion and debate, the steering committee ultimately narrowed the list to 10. Then after more animated discussion, they recommended five priorities for consideration by the council. When the council met in the summer of 2011 to review these five, a lively discussion followed. There was considerable pushback on limiting the priorities to just three, but the council co-chairs, staff of All Hands Raised, as well as Mayor Sam Adams strongly argued for focusing on a few critical priorities at the outset. Agreeing with this rationale, the council conducted a vote, and three of the five priorities rose to the top.

Ultimately, all of the key working groups involved—the board, council, steering committee, and data team—reached a critical milestone when three initial priorities were selected to guide and focus collective action moving forward with three priorities: (1) eliminating disparities in children and youth success, meaning addressing the achievement gap with intentional focus on racial and ethnic disparities; (2) linking community and family supports to children and youth success, meaning improving the alignment and impact of extended learning opportunities as well as social supports; and (3) ensuring that all students enter school prepared to learn, focusing on early childhood education as a jumping off point for later success.

On September 9, 2011, the work to establish a council and ready the community for a new way of working together was affirmed when Oregon governor John Kitzhaber addressed the council along with 150 other community leaders about his vision for statewide education reform and the connection between work at the state level and the work that was being done in Portland and Multnomah County:

> Together, through Cradle to Career, you are demonstrating the power that a framework informed by credible and agreed-upon data and focused on student results can have in galvanizing a community to support all students. . . . The fact that so many of you are here today and involved in this work is a testament to our shared determination to deliver the right kind of support for our students—so that every one of them succeeds.[3]

The Work Begins

Early in 2012, the All Hands Raised Partnership established three additional collaboratives joining Ninth Grade Counts that brought together diverse stakeholders to address the three priorities through the development of specific shared goals, agreed-upon outcomes, and action plans to meet these outcomes. A co-convening partner with considerable experience relative to the area to be addressed organized the work of each collaborative. To guide the establishment of initial collaboratives, a Request for Qualifications (RFQ) was developed. This RFQ underscored that each collaborative had to be committed to shared outcomes reported regularly to the community, shared decision making, shared accountability, and must hold a deep commitment to continuous improvement.

To keep everyone on the same page and moving forward, a brief list of commitments that clearly defined each collaborative member's role and responsibilities, including sharing knowledge and resources, was developed. In addition, convening partners signed a memo of understanding detailing their specific responsibilities, including financial commitments, and finally all members of the collaborative were asked to sign off on their shared action plan. All these formalities were intended to ensure that the work promised was being done collaboratively and with the intention of focusing on the three priorities established to guide the shared work of the community.

"Portland is a city that wants to collaborate," concluded Dan. "Our community really needed this initiative and really needed a structure to make sure all these meetings are focused on improving outcomes. We now convene with a purpose, and it's very important because this work is urgent. This is the civil rights issue of our time."

Given PSU's role in the earliest days of the work, and the university's steadfast commitment to seeing a cradle-to-career framework established in the community, the university published the first Report to the Community in the fall of 2010. This initial report outlined more than 40 indicators. Once the three priorities of the work were established, the data team began meeting regularly to analyze the 2010 report with the primary goal of focusing and strengthening the indicators to a more manageable set that could be impacted and measured annually through a set of targets that would be established.

Another key to Portland's work was keeping the communication between all of the groups and the greater community open and transparent. Without community buy-in, investors, parents, and providers can lose interest. Right after the November 30, 2010, meeting, Dan Ryan began sending out regular updates on the progress of the work to the community. "With a cradle-to-career initiative, communication is much more about the work and our progress," reflected Jeanie Marie Price, vice president of communication for All Hands Raised. "We need to keep everyone at the table, and to do that, we've become less about press releases and more about modeling who we are in terms of being humble and authentic and managing people's patience."

The Data Tell the Story

"The work has to be rooted in data, and yet we also have to constantly remind ourselves that behind every piece of data is a child," said Dan Ryan. He continued,

> We formed because we saw the numbers, and knew we could do something about the eighth/ninth grade transition, which was itself a key sub-indicator of high school graduation. So data become the first solution out of the gate. The challenge is evaluating the programs, how many credits did these kids have at the end of ninth grade, and how can we move that dial. Now that we're collecting the right data, we're showing significant increases in credit attainment at the end of ninth grade for students involved in Ninth Grade Counts compared to those who are not. It's exciting to have this accountability structure that brings us farther along.

The council established and charged the data team with providing recommendations regarding data collection, analysis, and reporting to the steering committee. Staff from All Hands Raised and Portland State University supported the work of this data team, which was ultimately the driver of the content for a "Report to the Community." This included reviewing and updating the indicators. It also integrated school district "milestones" into the data framework and provided an interpretation and discussion on the indicators that would be presented in the report.

A second major responsibility of the data team was to establish effective data protocols for the emerging collaboratives. A member of the data team was appointed to work with each of the four collaboratives, as appropriate, to identify data related to demographics, best practices, and outcomes. Members of the data team established a collaborative process for networks to share and report data. Finally, they explored systems/opportunities for linking and aligning student data systems.

Data team members appointed to support the respective collaboratives assisted members in their early-stage work to quantify problems the collaborative intended to address. For example, the Communities Supporting Youth Collaborative captured the following as evidence of the lack of supports for students and families:

> There is a clear and consistent relationship between early school attendance and later achievement.[4] In Multnomah County, 20 percent of students in kindergarten through third grade are chronically absent from school, placing them at a significant risk of future academic failure. The numbers vary significantly by race: 33 percent of Pacific Islander, 31 percent of Native American, 30 percent of African American, 23 percent of Multi-Racial, 22 percent of Latino, 18 percent of White, and 9 percent of Asian students are chronically absent.[5]

Similarly, the Ready for Kindergarten Collaborative noted that once children enter school, data showed the following outcomes: Attendance in kindergarten is connected to academic success in later grades. In Multnomah County, 28 percent of kindergarten students are chronically absent from school (i.e., miss 10 percent or more school days). Black and Native American students, and students in poverty, are most affected.[6] And, 29 percent of students of color and 17 percent of white students in Portland's largest school district do not meet first grade literacy benchmarks.[7]

The Learning Laboratory: Ninth Grade Counts

In September 2012, the Northwest Evaluation Association released a report evaluating student-level impact correlated with participation in Ninth Grade Counts. The analysis revealed that academic priority students, those flagged as at risk of dropping out based upon a shared set of eighth grade early warning signs, who participate in Ninth Grade Counts, when compared to nonparticipants, earned significantly more credits in ninth grade (six credits compared to five), met the crucial on-track-to-graduate benchmark (six credits or higher) at a 12 percent higher rate, and had better school attendance by 24 percent.

It was clear that the collaborative approach was beginning to work, even in a small but measurable way. "Good will only gets you so far," said

Nate Waas Shull, vice president for partnerships for All Hands Raised. "Shared vision only gets you so far. People need to see concrete value to their organization and their work, and they need to see that we are in this together. Ninth Grade Counts has been a valuable tool for us in paving the way for the work of the other collaboratives."

Funding and Financial Support

From the beginning, it was Portland's business community that saw the value in creating a seamless education pipeline in the community. They also saw how the partnership's commitment to a continuous improvement discipline could drive community engagement and outcomes in a new and exciting way.

One of those corporations was JPMorgan Chase, a pioneering investor in the All Hands Raised Partnership, which provided critical financial support. Brian Stewart, community relations officer for JPMorgan Chase, commented on their investment, saying,

> The creation of a framework that specifically aligns programs to clear outcomes weeds out a lot of the ancillary programs that are out there. We are creating an opportunity for increased dialogue among funders. It allows local funders to concentrate on programs that are really moving the needle. We're on our way.

Terri Theisen, vice president for development for All Hands Raised at the time, reflected on the challenges of talking to potential funders about the cradle-to-career concept:

> When you present the idea of cradle to career to a funder, they look at you like you've lost your mind. They have no idea what you're talking about. They are focused on the outcomes, the measurables, the benchmarks. With this new big idea, we can make no promises about what those outcomes will be, what the percentages will be. You can only tell them that this is new—and we need something new, because what we've got just isn't working. Funders often want to see immediate progress, but you're just not going to turn around a failing education system

in five years. We are seeing progress, but it's not a silver bullet. There's a lot of patience when it comes to the environmental movement and replanting a forest—we're willing to wait ten years for that crop to reinvigorate, but when it comes to making long-term change in education or social services for our kids, we just expect it to be done now, and if in a year or two it doesn't happen, well then it's time for something new. It's incredibly challenging; some call it the microwave culture—we want to put something in, press start, and it's done.

Terri explained that the Portland corporate and nonprofit community was integral to the All Hands Raised Partnership, coming to the table not just with blank checks but with ideas and advice on how to better each step of the process.

I think anytime you come to private foundation funders with a big, bold education idea, they are a little shell-shocked right now. They've been burned before. They're healing and they want to make sure this isn't just another trendy silver bullet. And what's beautiful about this is that it's not.

All Hands Raised Partnership Today

All Hands Raised remains as committed as ever to building a collaborative learning support system from within the community. The partnership is taking action for bold system change, with public- and private-sector partners coming together—changing behaviors, practices, and culture—to collectively answer the question, "How can we improve?" We believe that this will ensure long-term, real results for our kids throughout their educational journey, from before school to the start of a career. The work of the four initial collaboratives continues with a focus on ensuring every child enters school prepared to learn, linking community and family supports to student success, and eliminating racial disparities. And, there are conversations underway now to establish a fifth collaborative focused on the high school to college and career transition in 2014.

The All Hands Raised Partnership has an early definitive win and is seeing the results they envisioned in 2010. The original collaborative, Ninth Grade Counts (NGC), is experiencing what is possible when aligned funding comes together with aligned practices. Members of NGC are focused on improving the transition into ninth grade, with a specific focus on impacting credit attainment, particularly for those students most at risk of dropping out. Our partners at the state of Oregon became interested in this work and its potential statewide impact. The Oregon Education Investment Board (OEIB) invited All Hands Raised to testify before the Ways and Means Committee where leaders from NGC shared the quality standards they are using to drive results across the community. Subsequently, the state established a grant to support efforts like these to keep targeted eighth and ninth grade students on track to graduate.

Eight NGC partners applied for this new state grant, and every one of them was funded. This is one example of how the effort is making progress in Multnomah County. As they expand the scope of the work, the partnership expects many more examples of how aligning practices among the many organizations in this community will leverage investments.

FAILING FORWARD LESSONS:
PORTLAND

- **BE READY FOR COURAGEOUS CONVERSATIONS.** So many aspects of this work require leaders to challenge the status quo, whether on operational issues like where the backbone should sit, or on community-wide issues like race, class, or culture.

- **DIVERSIFY INVESTMENT FOR THE BACKBONE.** Ownership for the backbone increases dramatically when multiple investors put resources on the table.

- **FOCUS, FOCUS, FOCUS.** It is easy to try to take on too much when you are "boiling the ocean" from cradle to career. Having the discipline to stay focused on a limited set of outcomes and related priorities is critical.

CHAPTER 5

Bridging Richmond

A Region in Transition

The greater Richmond area is a case study on the crippling impact of the Great Recession on local economies, exposing the cracks in the foundational beams that support their prosperity. Richmond, an intensely historic city in the heart of Virginia, has deep economic roots in agriculture, dating back to the colonial era when tobacco and cotton made Virginia the economic powerhouse of the South. Due to its financial prowess, Richmond attracted government power and investment, eventually becoming the capital of the Confederacy during the Civil War, a fact that even after Reconstruction led to heavy defense and government investment. Today, Virginia still has the highest defense spending of any state, and its economy is evolving toward a technology-centered model, hosting the highest concentration of tech workers of any state and focusing on data centers and computer chip production as its largest sources of income. The largest projected job shortages in the Richmond area include the major occupational groups of health care, business and financial operations, and computer and mathematical jobs, all of which provide above-average wages. This group of occupations is projected to grow fastest in the region by 2021.[1]

While these trends bode well for the region, it isn't all good news. The types of jobs that are developing are high-skill placements, requiring at least a bachelor's degree or intensive professional training. Compare this with the fact that only 31 percent of residents in the Bridging Richmond region hold a bachelor's degree or higher, and 28 percent hold only a high school diploma, and the rising skill gap becomes obvious. Without the proper educational foundation, it will be impossible for the residents of the greater Richmond area to benefit from this new economy. Conversely, Richmond will not keep up with demand without an educated, talented workforce.

Already, the region suffers from serious unemployment nearing 12 percent, compared to the national average of 10 percent. Median household income also suffers at an average of $39,608,[2] approximately $10,000 below the national median. More than 25 percent of Richmond residents have lived below the federal poverty line in the last 12 months, with the poverty rate for children under the age of 18 nearly double the national rate.

Richmond stood at a crossroads; as their economy modernized and grew, they were quickly approaching a shortage of talented workers and an excess of underskilled, undereducated residents, as their businesses neared the point of being unable to deliver on demand. It was the making of a perfect economic storm.

Economics Meet Education

The region's leaders were painfully aware of this grim economic outlook. Business, philanthropic, and education leaders had been reading the writing on the wall and struggling to piece together a solution, but no one was quite sure how to fix this cyclical problem.

Virginia Commonwealth University's Eugene Trani had been president for almost two decades and had committed a significant part of his tenure to ensuring VCU properly served the greater Richmond area, making it both part of the college's mission statement and a part of their day-to-day operations. Within his leadership team, Dean Bev Warren of the School of Education began researching ways in which the School of Education could better serve Richmond. An educator herself by training, Bev knew that VCU's 3,800 education students needed to be more involved in the educational landscape of the community, both for their own benefit and for the community's. Eugene Trani was a founding member of Urban Serving Universities (USU) and so was well aware of the StriveTogether Framework and the Living Cities grant.

Getting Started

The School of Education pulled together a proposal and was picked in early 2009 to be one of five sites nationally to become proof points. After this initial investment from USU, Bev sought financial support from local businesses in the greater Richmond area. Altria, the holding company for Philip Morris, is headquartered in Richmond and invests heavily in the community, so naturally Bev requested a meeting to discuss the possibility of strategic investment.

When she met with senior officials to describe the project and appeal for financial support, she discovered that they had recently invested in a program called Ready by 21, another education initiative aimed at improving the outcomes of children in urban areas, which had also recently picked Richmond as one of their new project sites. Undeterred, Bev managed to gain support from Altria, Richmond Community Foundation, and the Jessie Ball DuPont Foundation, and gain the attention of many of Richmond's business, industry, philanthropic, community, and education leaders.

Bev then took the Framework to community leaders in Richmond, asking them to join the executive council, the CEO-level board that would convene to make decisions about how to move forward. Among the solicited parties was Yvonne Brandon, superintendent of the Richmond Public Schools. Yvonne recalled,

> We were all in separate silos talking about essentially the same thing . . . I was dealing with someone about early childhood education and the programs generated by the United Way; Bev and I were talking about higher education and K–12 alignment; so when someone called me and said we're having this meeting about the possibility of blending or bridging all of these concepts and putting them in sequential order so that we can all have the same type of conversation about something that is really badly needed in this city, I had to jump on the chance to attend.

Other founding members of the executive council included the presidents of the local chamber of commerce, the community foundation, the local community college and private college, as well as a multitude of executives from national corporations, including Capital One.

The group began meeting regularly, having frank discussions about how the education problem was leaking into the business community's ability to hire qualified professionals and how the school system needed resources to provide student support outside of school. With diverse voices at the table, it became clear that it was an issue on everyone's mind, and an overarching, comprehensive solution was needed.

After a few meetings, the group saw a presentation by CEOs for Cities, a global partnership that connects urban leaders to each other to disseminate innovative solutions for cities, in the same vein as USU but focused on benefiting the businesses that thrive in healthy cities. CEOs for Cities had come to Richmond to talk about Talent Dividend, a project that aims to raise the college attainment rate in the nation's top 51 metro areas by 1 percent. For each percentage point raised in college attainment rates, CEOs for Cities estimates, per-capita income goes up $856. If college attainment were raised by 1 percent in the nation's top 51 metro areas, it would mean an additional $143 billion in personal income per year nationally.

This provocative new lens to view college attainment hit a nerve with many around the table. Superintendent Yvonne Brandon remembered,

> I was interested in a lot of the things that CEOs for Cities had to say, but the fact that raising our college attainment by 1 percent equaled 9 or 10 million dollars in our region—that was an eye opener . . . I just knew it was a lot of money, and it's an investment we can do and just move the needle a little bit to get to that 1 percent. I left thinking, I wonder what would happen if we moved the needle in giant steps?

With excitement running high, and the right players at the table, Bridging Richmond felt ready to launch.

A High-Profile, Fragile Start

In July of 2009, the partnership called a press conference to publicly announce its formation. Richmond's biggest names turned out, as did the press corps. The area's newspapers and TV stations lined up to hear the groundbreaking announcement of unprecedented collaboration around the region's most pressing education issues. The media event garnered much attention, with high-level officials from the education, business, and philanthropic sectors under the media spotlight pledging their time and effort to this new partnership.[3] The resounding positive press coverage caused a buzz in the city, with enthusiasm and excitement abounding. But this wouldn't last long.

Weeks later, Eugene Trani retired. After more than 18 years at the helm of Virginia's largest university, Trani left VCU's leadership to Dr. Michael Rao, who took over as president in 2009. Further, Bridging Richmond experienced a transition when the partnership's first executive director, who had helped pull together the executive council, also left. Meanwhile, in the spring of 2010, Bev Warren transitioned from dean of the School of Education to interim provost for the university.

A second executive director was hired in the summer of 2010, one with a considerable background in education, having previously worked both with K–12 and higher education. But having an education-heavy background posed challenges for effectively communicating with and engaging the noneducation stakeholders at the table. The council began to lose momentum, and members began skipping meetings or sending their second- and third-tier staffers. According to John Easter, senior vice president for government and community affairs at the Greater Richmond Chamber of Commerce,

> There was substantial concern about the effectiveness of this organization . . . A lot of key business leaders who were brought on early and participated in some of the executive committee council meetings got quite frustrated that progress wasn't being made towards the goals. Everyone recognized they were worthy goals, but I think a lot of concern was around can we get it operating efficiently and be making progress towards these goals in a way that makes sense to people.

By the end of 2011, the second director stepped down, and it was time to take a serious look at Bridging Richmond's challenges, its relevance, and future direction.

Leadership and Organizing Framework for Bridging Richmond

Nineteen influential individuals and organizations made up the Bridging Richmond executive council, including the presidents of Virginia Commonwealth University, the University of Richmond, Virginia Union University, J. Sargeant Reynolds Community College, and John Tyler Community College and the superintendents for Richmond, Chesterfield, Hanover, and Henrico public schools. The council also included business and civic leaders from the Altria Group, Dominion Resources, Capital One, and Genworth Financial and the heads of the United Way, the Virginia Early Childhood Foundation, the Greater Richmond Chamber, and Community Foundation.

With VCU as the anchor organization, members of the community felt as though the partnership could be trusted and was rooted in transparency and accountability. As Cathy Howard, vice provost in VCU's Division of Community Engagement, said,

> What's really nice about Bridging Richmond is that it brings four major school districts together, and those superintendents are now working very well together. They are recognizing that the problems that used to be just the city's are now being felt in the counties, and having community colleges on board is also very helpful.

Action Teams Structure

The executive council, through an operations leadership team and the director, provided guidance to *action teams* created to meet key goals for three major time periods along the education pipeline. Each action team focused on that particular time period as well as the important transitions between those blocks of time. The three time periods were identified as: (1) early years (birth through grade 3), (2) middle years (grade 3 through grade 8), and (3) young adult years (high school into a postsecondary and vocation). These action teams first identified the networks and programs that were already in place and to some degree addressing their priority goals. They also assessed existing networks and programs relative to their effectiveness in the context of what data and information was available. The next step was *aligning* and *coordinating* existing networks and programs, adding additional ones, and most importantly engaging the local community to drive action.

Bridging Richmond's Aspirational Goals

1. Every child will be prepared for school through high-quality early childhood education.

2. Every child will be supported inside and outside of school.

3. Every child will succeed academically.

4. Every young person will complete some form of postsecondary education.

Goal 1: Every child will be prepared for school through high-quality early childhood education.

In the greater Richmond region approximately one out of every six children entering kindergarten is identified as needing additional literacy instruction. This means that every year 1,700 children enter kindergarten in need of additional instruction in basic literacy skills. As a consequence of this lack of readiness, more than 1,550 students each year fail to meet even the basic-level requirements in reading at the third grade level. Early childhood education—preschool through third grade—provides the foundation for future learning.

A major learning outcome is the acquisition of literacy fundamentals, which are predictive of future reading success. The Early Intervention Reading Initiative was established in Virginia to help participating schools identify children in need of additional reading instruction and to provide early intervention services. Children who do not meet designated literacy benchmarks also receive help based on a statewide literacy screening called Phonological Awareness Literacy Screening (PALS). PALS is a measure of a child's knowledge of several literacy fundamentals including alphabet recognition, concept of word and sentence, knowledge of letter sounds and

spelling, matching literacy instruction to specific literacy needs and identifying each child's level of acquisition in these fundamental literacy skills.

A report released by Smart Beginnings Greater Richmond, a collaborative facilitated by the United Way of Greater Richmond and Petersburg and
the Greater Richmond Chamber, highlighted the successful implementation
of a regional kindergarten readiness and registration campaign, including a
single, shared registration date for 10 school districts.[4] This unprecedented
level of collaboration among local school districts resulted in 8,355 students
registering on time for kindergarten. Individual schools also reported that
more parents were better prepared with enrollment documentation. The
combined reach of the kindergarten readiness and registration message
from the public awareness campaign exceeded 3 million media impressions.

Through Smart Beginnings Greater Richmond, Bridging Richmond
was able to harness the momentum of early childhood stakeholders working
together as never before. Key conveners of the Early Years Action Team
are the United Way of Greater Richmond and Petersburg and the Greater
Richmond Chamber. An illustration of the impact of this coalition is in
the PALS-K indicator that measures knowledge of several important literacy
functions. The indicator illustrates the percentage of students identified for
additional instruction.

Goal 2: Every child will be supported inside and outside of school.

The quality and amount of support students receive both inside and outside
of school understandably influence their ability to succeed. This includes
social and emotional as well as academic support and involves working with
a variety of institutions. Children who receive the full spectrum of support
are less likely to drop out of school and more likely to be actively engaged
in their learning and achieve a sense of well-being. The cradle-to-career
interventions are distinctive not only in that they address critical touch
points in a more seamless fashion over an extended period, but that they
are focused on *out-of-school* factors as well as education within schools.

Tito Luna is the associate community development director for the
YMCA and a member of the operations leadership team. He also worked with
the Promise Neighborhood initiative in the East End and the partnership

for Out-of-School Time. While he has a history of working in collaborative efforts, he believes Bridging Richmond is different:

> First, the high-level folks are involved. A lot of times collabora-
> tives form because there's self-interest. But this is not the case
> here. It's everybody working together, breaking down silos, and
> true collaboration. Trying to find ways that we can *collectively*
> impact our communities. I've seen a lot of collaborative efforts
> form because a certain pot of money was available, and then
> once that money dried up, there goes the collaboration. This
> isn't why people have come together here.

A common activity in cradle-to-career sites like Bridging Richmond is to examine helpful existing resources and enterprises, at times through structured processes called asset mapping. This is to offset a deficit orienta-tion and perspective. Harold Fitrer of Communities In Schools cautioned, however, that this process has to be comprehensive across the entire region to really understand what's going on outside of school:

> There's been a lot of previous asset mapping done, but they just
> haven't gone deep enough. For example, the United Way did an
> asset map on early child care in Richmond. The problem with
> it is that it came out and essentially said in Richmond we look
> great. There are a lot of quality early childhood programs. But
> go to the Promise Neighborhood area up on Church Hill and
> except for one program there's nothing else. It's like a desert. Most
> of these kids are being kept by a grandma, aunt, or a neighbor
> who has this as their job. They keep under seven kids because
> that way they don't need to get licensed. And you're not going
> to run them out of business because they're neighbors. We have
> no doctors on Church Hill. Practically none on the East Side
> or South Side of Richmond. But if you look at Richmond as a
> whole, we have more doctors per capita than most cities. That's
> partly because we have VCU as a teaching hospital here. As
> another example, we have all these middle school programs, but
> it wasn't until we started getting in the car and going to visit

them that we could get a really good assessment. It may be a great program, but there's only six kids in it!

Bridging Richmond focused on getting a better handle on out-of-school interventions and services and their quality and scope of effort. Through an initiative of the YMCA and United Way, and in partnership with the City of Richmond, standards for out-of-school services and interventions were developed. Tito Luna of the YMCA talked about forward progress with standards:

Since Bridging Richmond emphasizes standards and assessment, that's when we gained momentum, and I mean standards for *out-of-school* services as well as for kids who need a range of help and support. We are involved in a process to create such standards for the City of Richmond. We've had conversations with Michigan State Department of Education because they're ahead of a lot of other states in terms of standards for out-of-school time. We need to look at safety, staffing, active interaction with the kids, programming, and training for those who are providing services.

The Greater Richmond Youth Development Partnership (GRYDP) provided leadership for the Middle Years Action Team, which aids students from fourth to ninth grade. The partnership is dedicated to ensuring the region's young people are healthy, succeed academically and are socially and civically engaged. The partnership works to address key gaps in the quantity, quality, and consistency of services and opportunities for children and youth from kindergarten through high school. It operates within the localities of Hanover, Henrico, Chesterfield, and the City of Richmond. Key conveners of the Middle Years Action Team are the United Way of Greater Richmond and Petersburg and the YMCA of Greater Richmond. In 2012–2013, the GRYDP piloted training and continuous improvement for service providers to be used to scale up in the following year. The GRYDP has also been working closely with the City of Richmond to bring the development of quality out-of-school time standards to policymakers for implementation.

This process embodies the principle that everyone in the community has a stake in educational outcomes. Families need the support for their children and youth, especially if either parent works or a single parent has a full-time job or more than one job. The lead organizations involved include large community-based organization such as the United Way and the YMCA as well as small groups like FeedMore and the Peter Paul Development Center.

Goal 3: Every child will succeed academically.

Because student academic success was the *core* objective of all of the efforts of Bridging Richmond, the group collected baseline data through Virginia's Standards of Learning (SOL), which provides *criterion-referenced tests* designed to measure mastery of content through both annual tests and alternative assessments. Although it is the primary system of accountability in Virginia, SOL is only one of many indicators used to inform instructional decisions made by and on behalf of students.

Reading on grade level in third grade is an important measure of preparation for school, and reading below grade level often results in students not being promoted or long-term remediation.

As the final year of elementary school, fifth grade represents a key transition point in education. Achievement scores from this year provide an index of the skills students have acquired prior to entry into middle school and are used to determine instructional needs.

Eighth grade represents another key educational transition as the final year of middle school. The SOL test scores for this grade provide an index of the skills that students have acquired prior to entering high school. This critical transition year also serves as a key point in students' commitment to education. Academic difficulty at this point is a clear risk factor for dropping out of school.

In 2011, Bridging Richmond piloted the Student Gallup Poll in the Metro Richmond region. This web-based national survey captures the thoughts of students in areas related to hope, engagement, and-well being of students in grades 5 through 12 across the United States. Results revealed that 55 percent of students surveyed reported feeling hopeful, while 31 percent of middle school students reported being stuck, and 14 percent reported feeling discouraged. In the area of engagement, 62 percent of middle school students surveyed reported feeling "engaged" while 25 percent indicated they were "not engaged."

In the area of well-being, 67 percent of students reported feelings of "thriving" while 32 percent reported that they were "struggling." The plan is to administer this survey each fall and to utilize the data to determine areas where more students report being not engaged, stuck, or struggling so that interventions may be initiated to address the motivational level of middle school students.

The alignment of efforts for quality out-of-school time are relevant to this indicator and ensuring the youth are engaged, hopeful, and well. A few key partners were aligning their work in this area.

Goal 4: Every young person will complete some form of postsecondary education.

Successful completion of educational experiences beyond high school is becoming increasingly important to America's economic future. In Virginia, it is projected that 64 percent of all *existing* jobs (2.8 million) will require some training beyond high school, and 72 percent of all *new* jobs will require some training beyond high school by 2018. High school graduation rates in the region are continuing on a positive trajectory with a 2.6 percent increase over the baseline year (2010). The dropout rate for the region, using the federal definition, was 18 percent in 2010, a decline from 19 percent in 2009.

To examine first-to-second-year college retention rates, Bridging Richmond uses the Postsecondary Education Data System, which tracks the progress of students who begin their studies as full-time, first-time degree- or certificate-seeking students and identifies those who complete a degree or other award, such as a certificate, within 150 percent of "normal time" for completing the program in which they are enrolled. First-year retention rates for the three universities (Virginia Commonwealth University, University of Richmond, and Virginia Union) that participated in Bridging Richmond were reported at baseline (2009) and for the 2010 academic year. These institutions represent a broad spectrum of university classifications (private, large public, historically black college or university).

The retention rates remained stable for 2010 and ranged from 50 to 93 percent. Six-year graduation rates ranged from 87 percent (private university) to 32 percent (HBCU). Community college data reported those who earned one of three types of degrees: career technical, certificate, and college transfer. Certificate completions increased almost 30 percent from the baseline year (659 to 842), and degrees that position students for transfer increased 36 percent (667 to 909).

The Promise Neighborhood as a Community of Practice

Bridging Richmond and Richmond Promise Neighborhood adopted similar community indicators of success and are jointly managing a data system to track organizational and school efforts to best serve children and youth in the region. In a collaborative effort, Communities In Schools and VCU have partnered to purchase and manage a data system with demonstrated success in performance management within and across human service organizations. With CIS of Richmond as the fiscal agent and VCU as the neutral data manager, Bridging Richmond and Richmond Promise Neighborhood are piloting the use of the Results Based Accountability (RBA) methodology, software that links community indicators to performance measures and the strategies and programs that are working collectively to make progress. The partnership between Bridging Richmond and Richmond Promise Neighborhood has led to sharing resources, the development of a shared framework for continuous improvement, and the opportunity for Bridging Richmond to apply what is being learned at the neighborhood level to the region.

While the Promise Neighborhood proposal for East End Richmond wasn't funded, several agencies and individuals who developed the proposal are staying the course, and this provides a focal point for Bridging Richmond to build upon. As Harold Fitrer observes,

> The Promise Neighborhood proposal didn't get funded, but the group has stayed together . . . The local funders that were at the table throughout this entire process said we're going to leave our money on the table. Those people included community foundations, the United Way, and the Robins Foundation. We, CIS, are the lead agency, but we don't operate all the

Promise Neighborhood programs. We just happen to be the lead organization.

Support for Bridging Richmond

Katie Fessler, senior manager of corporate contributions for Altria (the holding company for Philip Morris), was a member of Bridging Richmond's executive committee. Over the years, she has had a multitude of experiences with community groups but viewed Bridging Richmond as something different that can truly united the community around education in Richmond. Katie recalled,

> When we heard about the StrivePartnership and the interest in the broader community in Richmond in applying for a grant to develop a similar framework and infrastructure, I found it to be directly in the wheelhouse of the way we were already thinking about the education pipeline at Altria . . . If you look at the governance structure, it has a wonderful multiplicity of voices of key people in decision-making positions who bought into the idea early and most importantly have stayed engaged. This has not been without challenges. The messy part of coalition building had to happen and understand what and where are the *grassroots* as well as the *grassroof* linkages. During all of that norming, storming, forming business, some folks thought it's just another program or another coalition, but it's really a coalition of coalitions. This is the way Richmond should transform its community planning: around outcomes for youth.

A Fresh Start

After nearly three years of too many meetings and too few results, Bridging Richmond found a new beginning by establishing a transition team, and with the support of a local consultant, Communitas Consulting, Bridging Richmond began a rescrubbing of its mission as well as a search for a new executive director.

At around the same time, VCU released its new strategic plan, entitled "Quest for Distinction: Discover, Impact, Success." The plan was divided into four main pillars: high-quality living and learning experiences, research excellence, commitment to human health, and community engagement and regional impact. Within the fourth pillar was the explicit commitment to "create university-community partnerships with a focus on the key targeted areas of K–12, access to health, and economic development," and Bridging Richmond was a key, regional strategy for VCU.

VCU backed up this commitment by moving the Bridging Richmond initiative from the School of Education to the Provost's Office, back under Bev Warren. This gave the partnership access to decision making, financial, and staff support.

By July 2013, having conducted a series of interviews and meetings with the transition team and other partners, backbone staff, and the community at large, the consultant submitted a report. This report laid out the achievements of the partnership, included the establishment of a *shared community vision*. From corporate CEOs to local superintendents, they all understood the ambitious regional outcomes and target goals.

However, the transition report also acknowledged that employees of the partner organizations did not understand the vision, and that internal communications between the partnership and its members were shaky at best. It raised the issue of missing voices at the table, such as local government; and highlighted the executive council's frustration at the lack of progress and the fact that they didn't understand their specific role in the project. The report also noted that it wasn't clear what the collaboration between Bridging Richmond and the Richmond Promise Neighborhood was, that there were significant gaps in coverage when it came to programmatic resources, and that there was no plan for investments and sustainability.

At the same time, Bev launched a national search for a new executive director. Learning from past experience, she knew this new leader would need to have a wide range of skills: ability to connect and coordinate with community members, ability to speak comfortably with educators about the educational outcome for students, ability to connect with CEO-level executives and speak to them in terms and processes they understood, and proficiency in data management and translation.

Once VCU's strategic plan and Bridging Richmond's transition report launched, it was clear that Bridging Richmond was back on its feet. After

seeing the progress that the partnership had made, Kelli Parmley, associate vice provost for planning and decision support, decided to apply for
the position and was hired as executive director in August of 2012. With
a background in public administration, higher education, and strategic
planning, Kelli fit right into the role and was able to hit the ground running with the multitude of relationships she had developed over the years.
According to Kelli,

> The thematic thing for me is that Bridging Richmond was put
> under such a series of transitions that really hindered our abil-
> ity to get this thing off the ground . . . Now that we've moved
> past all that, and learned what it had to teach us, I think we'll
> be making real progress soon.

FAILING FORWARD LESSONS:
RICHMOND

- **FIND THE RIGHT STAFF RIGHT AWAY.** The skills needed in an
  executive director for this work are unique. Take the time, working
  with partners, to identify the right leaders to establish the power
  of partnership.

- **LEVERAGE EXISTING WORK, BUT SET RULES OF ENGAGEMENT.**
  It is critical to leverage exisiting work, but it is also necessary to
  make sure partners understand what it means to engage with the
  partnership and what they can expect to gain in return (value exchange).

- **ESTABLISH A CLEAR CALL TO ACTION.** In this case, it was a
  struggle initally to motivate leaders, but the connection CEO's for
  Cites provided between education and economic development
  helped rally the community behind the cause.

CHAPTER 6

Seattle/South King County

The Road Map Project

While the Greater Seattle region boasts one of the best-educated workforces and strongest regional economies in the nation, for more than 55,000 low-income students growing up in South Seattle and South King County in the early 2000s, education results were shockingly poor. In 2009, community leaders began talking about working together in new ways to help the young people of South Seattle and South King County. In early 2010, they launched the Road Map Project with the aim of dramatically increasing student achievement from cradle to college and career. Today, hundreds of organizations, individuals, and a broad coalition of community groups are involved. The Road Map Project region covers seven school districts and five community colleges.

Inspiration for the Road Map Project came from a variety of sources. Many individuals and organizations in the Seattle area had become familiar with the work of Geoffrey Canada and the Harlem Children's Zone and liked the data-driven, holistic, cradle-to-career approach. On the recommendation of Living Cities, several Road Map Project education leaders went to Cincinnati, where they found the StrivePartnership's common set of indicators to be very instructive to the Road Map Project's start-up phase. Another major galvanizing force was the widespread frustration with system-level results despite years of hard work, generous philanthropy, and many model programs. The label "program rich but system poor" resonated among the early Road Map Project creators.

By 2012, the Road Map Project region was undergoing a dramatic demographic transformation. Fully two-thirds—79,000—of the K–12 students were nonwhite, making the area a strong "minority majority" region. The seven districts participating in the project were serving children from around the world, and more than 160 languages were spoken locally. This diversity of languages presented some instructional challenges, but the wealth of the region's global connections and a diverse bilingual population was also an incredible strategic asset. The region remained among the best educated in the nation, with 56 percent of adults in Seattle and 47 percent of adults in King County holding a bachelor's degree. But just one out of every four King County residents with a bachelor's degree or higher was born there. Talent is being imported, and local children continue to fall by the wayside.[1]

In addition to changing demographics, other trends were appearing across the Road Map Project region. Communities experienced a rise in poverty. Schools saw an increase in the number of low-income students. In the 2011–2012 school year, 70,000 students in the region were classified as low-income by qualifying for free or reduced-price lunch. Since the 2009–2010 school year, the number of homeless students has also increased by 30 percent—more than 700 students—to nearly 3,000 in the 2011–2012 school year.[2]

The Backbone Organization and Project Champion

The Community Center for Education Results (CCER) in South Seattle serves as the backbone organization for this cradle-to-career effort. Its primary functions include work group facilitation, communication support, data collection, analysis, and reporting, in addition to handling the myriad logistical and administrative details required to bring cross-sector players together on a sustained basis. CCER, a small nonprofit, is specifically designed to meet this daunting set of expectations and exists solely for the purpose of staffing and supporting the Road Map Project. The staff consists of 10 individuals serving the following core functions:

- Strategic leadership;

- Data analysis and reporting;

- Action plan development and implementation support;

- Community and parent engagement;

- Fostering aligned action and investment;

- Advocacy; and

- Communications.

Mary Jean Ryan is the organization's founding executive director. She is widely viewed as *the champion* and driving force for the Road Map Project. When asked about the start-up phase of the Road Map Project, Mary Jean recalled,

> The genesis of what eventually became the Road Map Project began to be seriously talked about in the summer of 2009. I served on the Washington State Board of Education and felt very frustrated by our state's lack of progress. I believed we had to try a new approach, one that was built from the community. Turns out many other people thought the same thing. The City of Seattle was interested in taking a very strong *outcome* approach for a new cradle-to-college special Families and Education Levy. Many Housing Authority communities were interested in planning Promise and Choice neighborhood projects inspired by the Harlem Children's Zone.
>
> Leaders at the Gates Foundation were also thinking about trying a new, comprehensive, community approach, as was former Seattle mayor and the Seattle Foundation's new CEO, Norman B. Rice; the chancellor of Seattle Community Colleges, Jill Wakefield; the Technology Access Foundation's executive director, Trish Millines Dziko; and many, many other nonprofit and community leaders. The stars lined up in a powerful way, and in January 2010, we created the Community Center for Education Results and dedicated staff for our new cradle-to-college and career partnership.

David Bley, director of the Pacific Northwest team at the Bill & Melinda Gates Foundation and a key leader in the establishment of the Road Map Project, reminisced about his organization's first involvement.

We began to ask ourselves, couldn't the Pacific Northwest team be clearer about what outcomes we were looking for, not only in the context of the foundation but also in the context of what the community tells us what they want and need? We shifted our portfolio into one of *thinking* and less grant-making for about a year, and in 2009, we started trying to figure out what is the problem that we are trying to solve and what it was going to take to solve it. We did not feel particularly constrained by how the foundation had done its work in the past. What popped out of that reflection and dialogue were the values and premises and assumptions that underlie what became the Road Map Project.

A Collective Effort Takes Shape

In Phase I of the Road Map Project, which was completed in 2010, initial baseline data were collected and the overarching goal was set: Double the number of students in South King County and South Seattle who are on track to graduate from college or earn a career credential by 2020 and close achievement gaps. Indicators of student success were identified to measure progress and had to meet four criteria: They had to be actionable, data had to be available, and they had to be understandable and meaningful. Multiple forms of community outreach were stated and conversations and convenings with potential funders initiated.

Participation from leaders in different sectors began to expand as CCER put forward the concept of bridging preschool, K–12, and higher education, as well as providing support for youngsters *out of* and *in* school. Four working groups were formed in 2010, each helping to identify key student success indicators. They were: (1) early learning, (2) K–12 education, (3) community supports, and (4) postsecondary success. In addition, the Education Results Network (ERN), a large body of concerned stakeholders from diverse sectors, was convened four times in 2010 to help inform the Road Map Project's initial efforts. ERN members provided feedback on key elements of the work, including the initial indicators and goals, and set the project's overarching goal. The initial Road Map Project was rolled out in December 2010 at a 500-person community conference attended by all of the region's mayors and school leaders.

The following figure shows, in the outer circle, the various cross-sector groups that work together in the Road Map Project to take *collective action* designed to result in *collective impact*. The inner circle represents how they have come together to form specific working groups, networks, and partnerships. For example, the K–12 school superintendents and community college

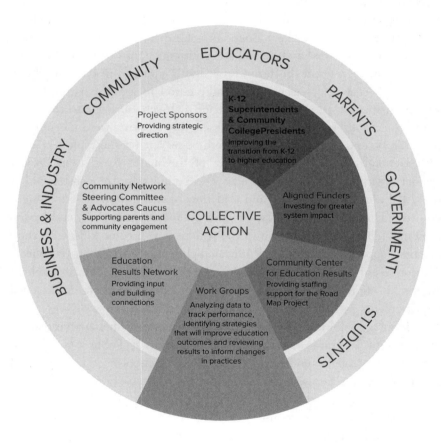

Road Map Project Collective Action

presidents meet on a regular basis as part of the Puget Sound Coalition for College and Career Readiness—something rarely done in regions across the country—to address how to improve college access and degree completion. CCER, as shared earlier, serves as the backbone staff for the Road Map Project. Aligned funders advocate for and work toward pooled or aligned investment across Road Map Project action plans and/or emerging strategic opportunities.

While leaders remained focused on long-term goals, all involved were aware that "early wins" were critical to demonstrate the power of taking a *collective impact* approach. Probably the best example from the early Road Map Project work in this regard was tackling the job of signing up students for the state's generous College Bound Scholarships, which promises tuition (at public tuition rates) and a small book allowance for low-income eligible students who sign up in the seventh or eighth grade, work hard in school, stay out of legal trouble, and successfully enroll in a participating higher education institution when they graduate high school. Prior to the Road Map Project's efforts, about half of the eligible students were missing this opportunity, and millions of dollars were being left on the table.

Deborah Wilds, a leader in one of the major Road Map Project partner organizations, The College Success Foundation, stepped forward at the 2010 kick-off conference and said they would initiate a serious sign-up drive. Hundreds of organizations and individuals joined in, and by the deadline, more than 90 percent of the region's low-income kids, with their parents' support, signed up and indicated they aspire to go on to college. This represents about 4,000 students and serves as an excellent example of an at-scale effort that can be leveraged by the project to get further needed improvements in college preparation, access, and success.

From a school leader's perspective, Josh Garcia, former assistant superintendent of Teaching for Learning for Federal Way Public Schools and current deputy superintendent for Tacoma Public Schools, said the successful sign-up drive was catalytic for the region. As Josh observes,

> The tremendous response to College Bound Scholarships is a classic example of how one expectation can rally seven different districts for a common cause and get results very quickly.

We still have to live up to that promise, but now we have kids signed up, kids aware, and how did that start? It was Mary Jean constantly saying, "Here's the progress," and it is really tied to what people want: their kids to be successful, to have that opportunity. It is not, "Wait a year for test results." It's, "Here's our goal. Here's the feedback continuously, and what are you *doing* about it?"

Cradle-to-Career Focus in and out of School

The Road Map Project's overarching goal is most important, as only 27 percent of ninth graders in 2000–2001 completed a postsecondary credential or degree by 2010 (2,254 college/credential completers from 8,448 ninth graders). While the Road Map Project endeavors to double the number of students completing college by 2020, emphasis is also placed on improving outcomes along the whole continuum. A cornerstone of the Road Map Project is a belief that supporting children's healthy development *at every age* is critical to their academic achievement and ultimate success in college and a career.

There is also an explicit commitment to closing the achievement gaps that affect many of the low-income students and students of color in the region. Gaps in readiness, achievement, and attainment among subgroups of students are apparent across the pipeline, and targets have been set for each major indicator with the ultimate aim of *eliminating* rather than reducing gaps.

To meet these goals, each district in the region goes at the work in its own way. The Kent School District, for example, offers free, full-day kindergarten to every student. To get an early start on reinforcing the importance of higher education, every kindergartner takes a field trip to a local four-year or community college. Within the district, the oldest students at Scenic Hill Elementary won't be ready to go to college for another 7 years; the youngest, not for 12 years. But every Monday, students and teachers at this Kent District school wear college T-shirts, the hallways ring with verses from college fight songs, and classrooms are festooned with more pennants than a university dorm room. To be sure, Scenic Hill Elementary has taken the college connection to heart. Inspired by California educator Damen Lopez's "No Excuses University," a project that encourages all students to aim for college, every classroom has adopted a college, and students and teachers wear that school's colors once a week. The school has also established "Parent University," offering parents basic math, English-language, and technology classes. That gives teachers another opportunity to talk to parents about sending their kids to college, too.

The Road Map Project recognized, however, that equal supports must surround children outside of school, and that they require better alignment and coordination between *out-of-school* services and interventions with reforms occurring *within* the formal educational structure. Frank Ordway, deputy director of the Washington State League of Education Voters, said,

> When people start arguing about why aren't all kids reading by third grade, the school people tend to react and say, "We can't do this on our own." They have a tendency to react negatively. One of the things the Road Map Project has done is shown that this responsibility is *shared*. We actually are partners in addressing these problems. It can't be overestimated how important this is because those in schools feel their budgets have been cut, their resources are dwindling, and they are under siege.

Community engagement, leadership, and initiative are central to the Road Map Project's vision and objectives. Mary Jean Ryan notes,

> In terms of community engagement, a central aspect of our game plan is that we need both an inside and an outside approach. We work with institutional leaders, but we must also work in *partnership* with our communities, and parents . . . We have to build up a stronger, feistier push to get improvement. It is largely kids of color who don't get the opportunities to succeed. Our community engagement strategy is very important to us, and we are working very hard on it.

She also underscored the importance of *community-level* outcomes, saying,

> They are essential. We can't continue with the program-rich/ system-poor scenario. We can't have twenty-five programs that are all declaring victory, while at the same time many, many kids are failing. Small subsets of kids are getting good programs, but the community-level impact is poor. Emphasizing the community-level context has been a big thing for us.

Ken Thompson of the Bill & Melinda Gates Foundation echoed this priority,

> We need a shared community belief in the importance of educational success. Early on, we said, "There needs to be outrage about the current state of things." Our leadership group consistently has said, "Don't come to this table if you don't have fire in your belly." I firmly believe we need broad community support to make change of this kind happen. That's going to make it a longer but stronger process, because we'll need that community support to get to our goal. One thing that seems unique to me about the Road Map Project is that it intentionally pursues both an "inside" strategy and "outside" system strategy at the same time. From day one, we said building on interest and concern in the community, mobilizing parents, and being able to exert external pressure on large systems has got to be a part of this work. My experience is that both kinds of engagement are needed to help make change happen in complex systems.

Aligning for Collective Impact

The Road Map architects have identified five major areas of work necessary for collective impact and improved student outcomes across the Road Map Project.

2020 GOAL

Improved Outcomes across Road Map Indicators

5

System Building Strategies and Actions

4

Aligned Action in School and Out

- Early learning providers
- Youth development organizations
- School districts
- Place-based projects
- Community Colleges
- 4-Year Institutions

1
Strong Data Results Reporting

2
Powerful Parent & Community Voice

3
Aligned Funding

Road Map Project Priorities

Guidelines for Workgroups

The workgroup should use the following set of common considerations to guide the process of identifying and recommending system-building strategies and actions:

- Effort has evidence demonstrating dramatic change in student outcomes.

- Effort has potential to significantly move Road Map indicators at scale.

- Effort has potential to significantly move Road Map indicators at scale related to achievement gap closure.

- Effort has potential to make progress quickly.

- Effort is aligned to key system partner's strategic plans and priorities.

- Effort does not need much, if any, new money.

- Effort can benefit from collaboration.

- Effort can benefit from community advocacy.

- Effort has a clear lead organization with the commitment and capacity to move.

Workgroups are asked to identify their priorities for consideration. These priority actions are extensively vetted. After priority actions are recommended and adopted, there are regular opportunities going forward to evaluate progress and refine or reset priority actions as needed to ensure that they reach the 2020 goal.

CCER also asks the workgroups to carefully consider the central matter of feasibility and asks each workgroup to address the following questions:

- Does the action have the support of system leadership (early learning leaders, K–12 superintendents, community college presidents)? If not, what is the feasibility of building support among system leaders?

- Are there existing funding and other resources to support the implementation of this action? If not, are there resources that could be reallocated from other areas?

- Does local and/or state policy enable adoption of this action? If not, is there political will for policy change needed to enable adoption? If not political will, is there public will needed to advocate for policy change?

- If these conditions are not in place in the Road Map region, what would need to happen for successful adoption and implementation across the region?

An external review of the Road Map Project by the Bridgespan Group in 2012 concluded that it had strong momentum as it moved more fully into a collective action phase. They identified five key elements as contributing to this momentum: (1) collaboration and competition, (2) creating the ideas of a (new) system, (3) leveraging the power of data, (4) achieving early "wins," and (5) effective leadership by the backbone organization.

Guiding Principles and Core Beliefs

Road Map partners are now working to expand community engagement, and support parent and youth involvement. They have established an Advocates Caucus to support adoption and implementation of relevant local and state policy change to support improved education at all phases of the road map. A small grants fund (with grants up to $5,000) has also been established to help support grassroots involvement in improving education. There is growing momentum, too, around *neighborhood-focused* efforts to improve education across the pipeline, in large part due to the success of the Harlem Children's Zone and the Promise Neighborhoods program in the U.S. Department of Education.

The Road Map Project is extremely supportive of the development of these neighborhood efforts in South Seattle and South King County.

Building *local* commitment to improved education, cradle through college and career, is an essential component of building a broader movement for change in the region.

As Mary Jean and other leaders in the Road Map Project continue to meet on a regular basis. They use the following set of six guiding principles to drive their work:

1. *The focus must be on multiple points on a continuum, from preschool through postsecondary.* Taking a cradle-to-career approach enables seamless transitions along the education pipeline, reducing the number of students lost along the way and, at the same time, preserving achievement gains. Both school-based and nonschool-based efforts are necessary to improve student outcomes.

2. *The commitment has to be regional.* Change must happen for the entire geography of South Seattle/South King County.

3. *Full engagement from multiple sectors and partners must be stressed.* When significant numbers and a diverse array of stakeholders are involved from the beginning of a planning process and when they remain engaged throughout, the success rate for adopting system-building plans, creating institutional pressure, implementing strategies, and achieving *impact* improves. In order to successfully engage a large, diverse array of stake-holders over time, it is critical to be extremely transparent about all decisions and actions. Trust is key.

4. *External pressure and partnership are necessary.* While there is an inherent tension to using both "outside-in" (external pressure) and "inside-out" (internal approaches) strategies to improving education institutions, a combination of these models selected on a situation-by-situation basis is necessary to make change happen. Unusual alliances are encouraged to transform the status quo, and there is recognition that conflict is inevitable.

5. *Evidence and examples are essential.* Successful strategies exist that prove that students of all races, ethnicities, and economic backgrounds can succeed academically. Evidence-based practices need to be implemented and scaled; innovation also has to adapt to local contexts and situations where there is no clear evidence.

6. *Transparency and accountability are essential.* All aspects of the education continuum benefit from strong feedback loops and greater "consumer" awareness. It is imperative to establish common, transparent, and actionable metrics to gauge progress and enhance decision making. Further, there has to be willingness and flexibility to change quickly based on results.

The Road Map Project has also identified core beliefs about the region's students, including:

- Every student can learn and succeed.

- Expectations must be high for every student. Low expectations breed lower success rates.

- A component of creating change will involve building belief systems in our target communities about these core assumptions.

- Race and class issues permeate the educational disparities in our region. These issues must be acknowledged and addressed in order to drive change.

Keys to Success

A number of people spoke to the Road Map Project's promising beginning. Sili Savusa, executive director of the White Center Community Development Association and co-chair of the Road Map Project's Community Network Steering Committee, put it this way:

Communication is what makes it work. People need to check their egos around this work at the door. I don't care who you are. If you believe that every child deserves a quality education, that has nothing to do with your title. The question is what you are going to do to make that happen.

Similarly, Josh Garcia said,

Schools can't do it alone. I believe that most of the brick walls that our kids face are made out of human flesh. They're excuses. They're low expectations. But there needs to be some consistency in terms of high expectations. If we can influence the conversation to ensure that *every* kid is college-eligible when they walk out of their schools, then I can look myself in the mirror and say, "You know what? I earned my money today."

Mary Jean added:

The significant, multisector participation is probably our biggest strength. I have been amazed with the outpouring of people who want to do their part. They see that there is a bigger picture and that if they do their part and other people are doing theirs, then we might actually be able to do something really big. It is one thing to say, "We're collective impact. We're all going to be doing this." And it's quite another thing to actually do it and show them. The Road Map Project is very serious about *getting results*. We're committed to getting the job done. We are not happy with the state of affairs for kids in our area. We need much better educational outcomes and the traditional ways are not working successfully. It is a very serious collective effort to change educational outcomes by working on strengthening systems in a way that has not been done before. It is actually creating a new educational system.

FAILING FORWARD LESSON:
SEATTLE

SET A CLEAR AND COMMON GOAL. Even if it means lifting up a specific community level outcome above the others, this gives partners a unified target to work toward.

CHAPTER 7

Houston

All Kids Alliance

Greater Houston: Context and Challenge

All Kids Alliance in the Houston metropolitan area is distinct from the other three case studies in that it operates within an extremely large geographic area. As a way to accommodate this vast catchment area, the Alliance has adopted a "hub-and-spokes" methodology with a core group of staff focused on supporting specific subsets of the Greater Houston region. In working with the "spokes," the Alliance builds support and capacity for its regional partners in four primary ways:

- Recruiting members to regional executive leadership councils.

- Providing data and coaching for meeting priority targets.

- Ensuring continuous improvement and collective commitment through working collaboratives that identify change strategies.

- Fostering accountability and sustained pursuit of outcomes for kids, cradle to career.

All Kids Alliance is committed over the long term to creating cradle-to-career organizations in every region of Greater Houston, defined as eight Texas counties: Brazoria, Chambers, Fort Bend, Galveston, Harris, Liberty, Montgomery, and Waller. The eight-county reach of the Alliance constitutes the country's sixth largest metropolitan area. The 2010 census estimated a population of 5,891,999 for this region. This population constitutes almost one-fourth (23 percent) of the population of Texas and nearly 2 percent of the population of the United States.

This huge geographic footprint, with so many different partners to engage, has created significant challenges for the Alliance, generating several failing forward lessons that benefit similar large metropolitan areas interested in taking on this work.

How It All Started: The Evolution of All Kids Alliance

In the late 1990s, then-state demographer Steven Murdock predicted that Texas would become a third-world economy by the year 2030 if it did not educate larger numbers of children from all racial and ethnic backgrounds to high levels of achievement. Responding to his analysis and the expressed concerns of the legislature, the Texas Higher Education Coordinating Board (THECB) developed a comprehensive blueprint for action titled *Closing the Gaps* (2000). This report called for enrolling 600,000 more Texas students in higher education by 2015, a figure that was increased to 630,000 in the 2001 update. One of the strategies the THECB employed to reach their ambitious goal was encouraging and providing financial incentives for P–16 councils across the state.

The challenge of the *Closing the Gaps* targets inspired then-THECB member Laurie Bricker to convene community leaders in the Greater Houston area to address forming a P–16 council. Bob Wimpelberg, then dean of the College of Education at University of Houston, and now the executive director of the Alliance, observed: "Laurie rounded up the 'usual suspects' to examine what P–16 means and how to address it in Houston." Laurie Bricker recalled, "I was on the coordinating board, and I wanted my home community to be out front in this movement." Laurie went on to explain that during her time on the coordinating board,

> whenever they talked about student success, someone always blamed the K–12 system for not properly preparing students, but representatives from K–12 were not included in those conversations. As a former teacher and a former school board member, I felt the challenge to get everyone involved in seeking solutions rather than in placing blame.

After 18 months of meetings and discussions, the P–16 group that Laurie convened grew to about 50 people representing public and private early childhood education, the K–12 sector, institutions of higher education, nonprofit organizations, governmental agencies, businesses, parents, and students. This group decided to call itself the Greater Houston P–16+ Council. The "+" was added to underscore the likelihood that many careers will require advanced degrees or continued education beyond an undergraduate degree. It followed the guidance of THECB, and according to Laurie, "We began examining our local data and discussed potential joint projects and cooperative ventures across the community." Bob Wimpelberg was impressed. "This P–16 approach to addressing problems struck me as the most comprehensive that I had seen in all my years in education," he said. "So I raised my hand to volunteer to chair the original group."

The Greater Houston P–16+ Council adopted the following overarching goals:

- Be a recognized, convening collaboration of diverse stakeholders representing P–16 initiatives.

- Advance the systemic, comprehensive, and seamless alignment of educational and training experiences through an inventory of needs, opportunities, and replicable models.

- Promote a mindset among all children and parents that includes pursuing postsecondary education and training.

Donna Scott, associate executive director of the Alliance, recalled that council members

> eventually realized that a group of 50 people could not plan and carry out programming for more than a million students in a metropolitan area of 5.8 million people. So the council began to consider a role of creating, supporting, and connecting a web of local councils to do the "on-the-ground" work envisioned by the Greater Houston P–16+ Council. It helped launch such local councils to the west and southwest of central Houston and affiliated with existing groups with compatible visions.

Those first councils followed the THECB "P–16" model and in some cases received THECB seed money to advance their organizing efforts, but everyone continued to think in terms of projects and grants. These first P–16 councils had discussions about cooperating instead of competing for grants, about multidisciplinary approaches to problems, and about how to stop blaming one another for the community's problems. They also discussed how to share data that were often considered proprietary or confidential. Also, THECB encouraged state colleges and universities to organize *in-house* P–16 efforts, which generally focused on the high school to college transition and how to increase participation and success in these institutions.

Alliance Organization and Governance

After a few planning sessions around programming for educational change, the Greater Houston P–16+ Council realized that it was about to head into the same rut so familiar to many of its members, the design of "one-off" projects conceived with little knowledge of baseline data and undertaken with meager prospects for sustainability. Simultaneously, members of the P–16+ Council who were associated with the University of Houston began to hear about the StrivePartnership in Cincinnati.

To the project-wary P–16+ council, Cincinnati's deeply systemic work was highly appealing. Barely a year after it adopted bylaws and began to move into action mode, the Greater Houston P–16+ Council dissolved itself to make way for All Kids Alliance.

The implementation of the Alliance began under the leadership of University of Houston president Dr. Renu Khator, who chaired the original Alliance Council of Executives during its development and through its formal launch in June 2010. Laurie Bricker of Jeffries & Company assumed this leadership role shortly after the public launch and turned it over to Gus Noojin, retired president of Shell U.S. Gas & Power, in the fall of 2012.

The Alliance recruited a council of executives consisting of more than 30 members. The education sectors are represented by P–12 superintendents as well as college and university presidents. There is executive-level leadership from the United Way of Greater Houston, the Greater Houston Partnership, the Houston Hispanic Chamber of Commerce, the Houston

Area Urban League, the Gulf Coast Workforce Development Board, and the American Leadership Forum. Industry is well represented, with Chevron, CenterPoint Energy, Jeffries & Company, JP Morgan Chase, Deloitte and Touche, and AT&T all at the table.

Representatives from the nonprofit community are involved as well, including the executive directors of Houston A+ Challenge, YMCA, The Center for Houston's Future, Children at Risk, Raise Your Hand Texas, Communities In Schools, Project GRAD, Parents for Public Schools, and Neighborhood Centers, Inc.

Several other community leaders expressed interest and a desire to support the Alliance but could not commit to the time requirements. Those leaders were invited to join an advisory council, serving as ambassadors in the community and contributing professional expertise to the Alliance as requested. One advisory council member, a lawyer, offered the expertise of his firm's intellectual property department *pro bono* to help the Alliance with branding and filing its name with the federal registry. Another, a prominent corporate CEO, helped the Alliance gain visibility in the Greater Houston nonprofit arena.

Bob Wimpelberg served as managing director of the Alliance during the year after its launch. In May 2011, he stepped down from the deanship in order to lead the Alliance full-time as executive director. Dr. Robert McPherson, the incoming dean of the College of Education, has continued strong support for the Alliance and has allocated prime space to house the Alliance staff. The Alliance initially had a core backbone staff of four individuals, and a director of data services and research has since joined the staff. The Alliance staff is designed to remain small and focused on its primary role of encouraging the development of regional councils and to support these councils as they implement the StriveTogether Framework.

Managing Change in a Metropolitan Area: The "Hub-and-Spokes" Approach

The fact that the Alliance serves such a large geographic area and population meant that it needed to take a different path from the other cradle-to-career communities. The Alliance chose to be a *capacity-generating organization*—using the StriveTogether Framework—that would work with other organizations within the entire eight-county metropolitan area.

Current estimates are that the Alliance will eventually end up with 15 or more regional councils. In 2012, Alliance staff were in conversation with six different groups in different parts of Greater Houston, and day-to-day Alliance-based work was going on in two of those six regional communities.

The specific regions where the Alliance was holding conversations are in blue. As Associate Executive Director Donna Scott described it: "We

All Kids Alliance Hub and Spokes Model

have a kind of step-wise way that regional councils roll out, and it starts with recruiting the right membership to lead the process."

As the hub, the Alliance coaches regional advocates on how to develop an organization adapting the Framework to drive educational change. As a purveyor of "direct services," the Alliance helps regional councils monitor their development, capture and use data, and employ continuous improvement protocols to realize scalable and sustainable change.

Common Outcomes across Regional Partners

Providing data for the spokes

In the hub and spokes model, the Alliance assumes the role of helping build regional councils that will eventually function as stand-alone cradle-to-career partnerships. A major function of the Alliance is to help generate a sense of urgency among community representatives underscoring the severe challenges that their children and youth are facing. It then helps the community collect and organize data needed to make informed decisions, coaching the working collaboratives in the use of the continuous improvement process adapted from Six Sigma.™

The Alliance organizes datasets in three formats. One is large and comprehensive, providing nearly 40 indicators on the cradle-to-career continuum. This dataset was first introduced as a baseline report in 2010, covering over 50 school districts. A second dataset focuses attention on a more limited set of key outcomes, which are aligned with a dozen data points. And a third, the "leaky pipeline," follows students' progress beyond the seventh grade ending with a single significant number: the percentage of students who, given enough time, graduate from high school and complete either a technical certificate or degree program.

Creating a baseline report

The Alliance baseline report includes nearly 40 cradle-to-career data points along with several *quality of life* statistics. The Alliance is committed to track these data points every year for Greater Houston and to disaggregate them for each of the regional councils. But learning to use data to tell the story is challenging. Pam Campbell, an administrator in the San Jacinto College District, involved in start-up planning for the Monument regional council, pointed this out with the following example:

> The Alliance annual report provides student achievement scores. In Texas, these scores (known locally as the TAKS scores) are reported in terms of "passing" and "commended." The passing numbers are widely publicized, and for most school districts the passing rates appear quite respectable. However, what parents often do not realize is that only the commended score means the child's test results indicate a readiness to move to the next level. Sadly, there is a huge gulf between most school districts' passing and commended reports.

The leaky pipeline: a single indicator

The Alliance is ultimately attracted to a single data point originally developed by the research staff at the Texas Higher Education Coordinating Board. This data point involved tracking a "pipeline" of seventh graders through high school to postsecondary access and success and measuring the "leakage" along the way. The single number generated in this approach is the percentage of students who eventually earn either a certificate or academic degree, given enough time to do so.

Common Outcomes across Regional Partnerships

When the Alliance staff presented its 2011 update of the 2010 baseline report to the council of executives, Gus Noojin suggested narrowing the focus to a few more powerful indicators to generate a clearer message. This prompted the council of executives to organize and prioritize the 40-point data system into a dozen "key outcomes." The purpose of the key outcomes is to serve as north stars or a constant reminder for all council members— and their communities—of their long-term direction and goals for their kids. The Alliance staff is benchmarking each key outcome as illustrated in the following figure.

Key Outcomes

Adopted by All Kids Alliance Council of Executives—January 26, 2012

Alliance Goals "All children/ youth ready for . . ."	Key Outcomes	Indicators/Metrics	Bench-marks	Notes
School	Sufficient readiness by kindergarten Pre-literacy Pre-numeracy	Percent "promoted" from 1st to 2nd grade	TBD	Several assessment systems are used across Greater Houston without much consistency in where they are used or what they measure
Middle School	Proficiency- 3rd grade: reading* 5th grade: reading* math*	Percent scoring at "commended" level or equivalent on state exams (currently TAKS)	TBD	Source: Texas Education Agency
High School	Proficiency- 8th grade: reading* math science	Percent scoring at "commended" level or equivalent on state exams (currently TAKS)	TBD	Source: Texas Education Agency
College	Completion of High School and Profiiciency- 11th grade: reading* math science	Percent of 9th grade cohort graduating with high school diploma in four years; percent scoring at "commended" level or equivalent on state exams (currently TAKS)	TBD	Source: Texas Education Agency; The content indicators will change when new STARR system is implemented; SAT/ACT data may also be used
Career	Completion of internship/ apprenticeship program,certificate program, or degree program	Percent of post-secondary population completing internship/ apprenticeship, technical certificate, associate's degree, or bachelor's degree in time-appropriate manner	TBD	Source: Texas Higher Education Coordinating Board—Rates of completion of technical certificates and academic degrees
Life	Social-emotional development/ competence at key stages, preschool through post-secondary	To be determined	TBD	Good indicator systems yet to be identified; will range from early development to workplace "soft skills"

Establishing Action Steps to Create Regional Councils

After soliciting feedback from a wide variety of stakeholders across Greater Houston and incorporating lessons from other cradle-to-career sites, the Alliance articulated a set of steps for developing regional councils:

- First, a regional council is formed with multisector stakeholder leaders working together for their children and youth.

- By studying data that illustrate children's needs, the council establishes a set of "north stars," 6 to 10 key outcomes that will guide their work over the next several years.

- Next, using achievement data as well as awareness of the community assets already in place to address those needs, the council identifies one or two initial "priority outcomes" around which work groups are formed.

- The council next recruits and helps develop the work groups, variously called "community action networks" or "collaboratives" for addressing each priority outcome.

- An action network or collaborative is coached by the Alliance in using a continuous improvement process to identify strategies supported by evidence-based best practices. The continuous improvement processes are adapted from Six Sigma.

- These improvement strategies are recommended to the regional council leadership by the networks. The regional council endorses the strategies and, with the help of the network, implements them.

Over time, each community action network (or collaborative) monitors the effects of the intervention. It modifies strategies when needed and will eventually turn it over to a willing and committed community organization as appropriate. As its capacity to support more action networks builds, the regional council moves more key outcomes into priority status and organizes a network or collaborative to address each outcome.

The West Houston Regional Partnership Experience

Mary Grace Landrum was the organizing chair and longtime member of the West Houston P–16 Council. She had been an original member of the Greater Houston P–16+ Council and was an early advocate of moving to the StriveTogether Framework and a hub and spokes model. She had spurred the formation of the West Houston P–16 Council, and she felt her council members were committed and eager to work.

Describing the West Houston group's relationship with the Alliance, Mary Grace explained,

> We got organized and the Alliance disappeared. We followed the guidance of THECB to recruit representatives from all the sectors in our area. We adopted bylaws. We got a grant to support committees working for change. We listened to Alliance presentations about this new framework and truly thought we were totally in line with the new thinking. Then the Alliance came back to us with further elements of the model and more new language. We were worried the Alliance would cause us to start over.

It turns out that as Alliance staff learned more about the Framework, they came to realize the critical importance of involving executive-level leaders of all sectors in full and active membership on the council. The West Houston Council had been engaging its school district superintendents only once a year as advisors. Also, the West Houston Council had not recruited executive-level members from the business community, organizing around mid-level employees instead.

Then there was the problem of vocabulary. Within a two-year time period, All Kids Alliance suggested that the West Houston Council refer to its "committees" as "community action networks," and before the dust could settle, the Alliance said that it preferred to call these groups "collaboratives." Again, the West Houston Council worried that the messaging signaled a need for them to start over.

As Bob described it,

> The West Houston P–16 Council was busy doing purposeful work. They had a regular and faithful attendance at their meetings; they commissioned committees to address council members' concerns and organized projects around those concerns. However, we soon realized that key elements of the StriveTogether Framework were missing. For example, they had recruited mostly middle-level organization people, not "executives." Further, learning to use the continuous improvement processes was not especially attractive to a group who convened to "get something done." They were meeting without the benefit of the kinds of technical assistance the Alliance staff had received from StriveTogether.

It took some time for regional council members to understand and agree with the Alliance about the importance of recruiting and fully engaging *executive-level* leaders. Tracy Janda, a community relations officer with CenterPoint Energy, is a member of the West Houston P–16 Council. Reflecting the spirit behind the THECB model for P–16 councils, Tracy recalled,

> I first joined a regional council thinking it would be a medium for promoting communication among the various community sectors serving children . . . I had experienced those in higher education not being aware and appreciative of the point of view of K–12. Also, the K–12 people were not talking to the pre-K service providers, so it was a blame game instead of pulling people together to address issues.

After becoming more familiar with the Framework, Tracy and the West Houston council began to see the full potential of a cradle-to-career framework as much greater than improving communication across sectors and role groups.

Over time, the Alliance realized that it could use its own council of executives to recruit regional leaders. Harriet Wasserstrum, president of American Leadership Forum, put it this way:

The Alliance Council of Executives represents leaders from every aspect of Houston life. We can identify outstanding individuals, often in our own organizations, to join these regional councils. Our role is more than just monitoring. I think if you look around the table at the council of executives, a lot of us are in positions to be able to help staff the regional councils.

A Revised Strategy Going Forward

The learning from West Houston councils helped bring about a turning point in the Alliance's development. Bob remembered how this experienced moved the work forward:

We needed to slow down, get to know our communities in depth, and help them build on what they already had in place. This meant that we would be working with two or three communities intensely instead of the up to 15 we had initially proposed. If we were serious about "taking the councils where they were," we had to approach the StriveTogether Framework out of sequence. We needed to consider, doing "on-the-ground" collaborative action before we recruited the full cohort of executive leaders we thought their council should have. This also meant viewing our work with the councils not so much as a "retrofitting" but as "building on their strengths."

At the same time as it plans to meet communities "where they are," the Alliance has learned that it must directly and fully communicate the fundamental shifts in strategy and organizing that come with undertaking this work. For example, all of its partnership sites started with minimal or multipurpose management. That is to say, day-to-day supervision of council activity was left to someone whose primary job was not directly related to council formation and development.

Skeletal management has slowed progress in these sites and has created challenges around keeping both the host organization and its council leaders engaged. Fortunately, this is changing. Two of the Alliance's affiliated councils now have dedicated managers, and the pace of progress in those communities is palpable. Equally encouraging is the fact that one of the Alliance's probable new sites has decided not to proceed on its accountability structure or community data work until it has secured two years' salary for a partnership director. Lesson learned: Someone needs to be waking up every day with a singular focus on laying foundational tiles on the path toward collective impact.

The Alliance has also wrestled with its own role as the "hub" in this model. Alliance staff now ask themselves, "Are we truly serving as training wheels or might we be developing codependencies with our regional council partners?"

Asking this question has caused the Alliance to clarify expectations for those who sponsor regional councils. There's more serious talk, now, about what it will take for a regional council to garner a level of local support allowing it to become independently sustainable. That means earlier conversations about regional council business plans and a funders' table. Ultimately, it means understanding that the most significant early milestone for a regional council will be gaining membership in the StriveTogether Network on its own. For All Kids Alliance, the lesson being learned is that the only meaningful marker of success in a "hub-and-spokes" arrangement is when the "spokes" can meet all of the benchmarks required for network membership without overly relying on the "hub."

What does the future hold for Greater Houston and the Alliance? The ultimate goal remains the same: That every child in Greater Houston will be represented by a regional council. The Alliance still estimates that this will require up to 15 regional councils across the 8 counties.

At present they are in various stages of conversation and/or direct coaching with nine regional groups. These groups serve approximately one-third of the children, cradle to career, in the entire Greater Houston area, so they are still extremely ambitious. The Alliance staff now is acutely aware that they cannot take a preexisting organization back to "square one" and move it from "partnership building" to "targeted outcomes" to "collaborative action." They now see that their very first step in working with a new community is to convince a community of the value of the Framework. This involves presenting compelling data and illustrations. They now also have an array of tools as well as expertise to offer each community group as it expresses interest in joining the Alliance.

Next Steps

Since we gathered information in Greater Houston for this chapter, the Alliance has continued to grow and put in practice the lessons learned from its start-up years. It continues to build local regional councils, being engaged with nine local conveners and in conversation with three others.

The Alliance also continues to use its dual approach to council building: in some cases, starting "from scratch" in a step-wise fashion and in others "jumping ahead" to do action collaborative/network processes before bringing the cradle-to-career organization fully into the StriveTogether Framework. The step-by-step work results from Chancellor Richard Carpenter of the Lone Star (Community) College System encouraging his six campus presidents to sponsor a P–16 effort and consider using the Framework for that process.

Three of the six campuses have set their leadership tables and have already reached the milestones of adopting a set of educational outcomes to guide their work and prioritizing specific outcomes for action.

In a regional partnership that encompasses most of Fort Bend County, the Alliance is facilitating a Collaborative Action Network with the intention of proving to influential community members that education forces can align around a shared outcome and arrive at promising strategies for change.

The value exchange that supports the Alliance's relationship with these four sites is an agreement by the Alliance to coach them throughout the start-up stages and provide services around data and continuous improvement. This was made possible by the United Way of Greater Houston, which financially underwrote the initial hiring of a director of data services and research.

From its regional councils, the Alliance expects three contributions: (1) that regional planners convene a leadership table committed to the Framework, (2) that they identify an "anchor entity" to support the work in their community, and (3) that they provide the initial staff member—a project director—to handle logistics in coordination with the Alliance. The Alliance makes clear the expectation that its role is to build capacity in the regional council for two years, after which the council will be "a boat on its own bottom."

Meanwhile, the Alliance has been busy creating tools around communications and process sequencing to assist in its efforts. The Alliance also continues to get technical assistance from StriveTogether and adapts, where possible, its local tools to national standards. For example, their "Progress at a Glance" charts were redesigned to align with the Theory of Action.

Importantly, the funding for All Kids Alliance has now found a broader base. When information for this chapter was gathered, support from the University of Houston (in kind) and from private foundations (through grants and gifts) constituted the lion's share of its resources. In cumulative terms, each of those two sources accounted for half of the Alliance's funding. In the past year or so, a successful corporate campaign has moved that sector to about a quarter of the financial support needed to maintain the Alliance.

Every year, All Kids Alliance becomes more broadly known in Greater Houston. Prospects are good for its controlled and steady permeation of all eight counties and for "collective impact" to enter common parlance in Greater Houston.

FAILING FORWARD LESSONS:
HOUSTON

* **EXECUTIVE LEVEL LEADERSHIP ENGAGEMENT IS CRITICAL.** In a large metropolitan region, it is even more important to have the right CEO level leaders engaged to work effectively with diverse communities across a broad footprint.

* **SIMPLIFY THE COMPLEX.** It is critical to make the work manageable to local stakeholders while not dumbing it down so much you lose the rigor.

* **START SLOW TO GO FAST.** Taking on too large of a geographic footprint or strategic focus too fast can actually put up more roadblocks than necessary.

PART III

Creating a Community of Practice

CHAPTER 8

Lessons from Winning Big
and Failing Forward

Based on the work of the four sites featured in the case studies and the broader membership of the StriveTogether Network, a host of key lessons are emerging as all the sites "fail forward" to build a new cradle-to-career civic infrastructure. The best way to capture the most critical lessons to date is by categorizing them according to four pillars in the Framework for Building Cradle-to-Career Civic Infrastructure outlined in chapter 2. Over time, we will be able to share lessons tied to each of the quality benchmarks outlined in the Theory of Action, which should help communities avoid key mistakes and build on local success to expedite their progress.

It must be noted that none of these lessons can replace the most critical ingredient in making partnerships successful: *trust*. Mike Soika, executive director of Milwaukee Succeeds, captured this in a simple statement as they struggled to organize their efforts very early in the work: "I have come to realize that partnerships move at the speed of trust." This could not be more accurate. In the end, this work—as is the case with all efforts that require people to change the normal way of doing business—must be built on strong relationships grounded in trust.

The following lessons related to common purpose and clarity will help build this trust. But in the end, it will take people willing to walk arm in arm to forge a new path to make this work stick over the long term. Cradle-to-career civic infrastructure simply will not emerge without such commitment. We cannot overstate the importance of this basic condition for success.

Framework Pillar I: Shared Community Vision

Two lessons have emerged and shaped the work of sites related to the first pillar of the Framework for Building Cradle-to-Career Civic Infrastructure. The first relates to establishing a sense of shared ownership for the work among all necessary cross-sector partners. The second is focused on cultivating clarity across all these partners about decision making, while ensuring that the process is both top-down and bottom-up.

Lesson One: Shared accountability, differentiated responsibility

As the work emerged very early on in the first cohort supported by Living Cities, the lead partners from all the sites got together and tried to put words to the struggles they were having in communicating this work. This has become a common refrain nationally, and as a result, StriveTogether has developed a toolkit with lessons, templates, and examples of how this can be done effectively. First, we needed a way to get at the ethic of what we were trying to establish together with sites nationally. Ken Howey, a key partner in Cincinnati and now across New York State, captured this beautifully: "We are trying to help partners realize they need *shared accountability* for results from cradle to career, even though there is *differentiated responsibility* across the continuum."

Rather than having partners from across sectors point fingers at each other and blame their peers in other sectors for the challenges we face, we needed to create a sense that moving the dial in the right direction is an exercise in interdependence. John Trever, former editorial cartoonist at the *Albuquerque Journal*, who got involved in a local partnership called Mission:Graduate, captured the challenge we are facing in the image opposite. Instead of pointing fingers, we need locked arms, walking together and working together with common purpose. And make no mistake: This requires transformational leadership. Put simply, we must have leaders who will stand up and model what it means to embrace a shared vision with equal passion and vigor as they advance their own mission within it.

© 2013 John Trever, *Albuquerque Journal*, reprinted by permission.

Nancy worked hard to model this in two ways: First, she found a way in any presentation related to education in the region to work in the StrivePartnership and what it stood for, along with how the work of the University of Cincinnati fit into this vision. This action spoke volumes to her peers and the community as a whole. Second, she demonstrated shared vulnerability. In one meeting, she stood up and made clear that UC faced a significant challenge with graduation rates, just as the school districts did. She acknowledged ownership of the outcome while asking for the partners' support. You could feel the superintendents, who often become the scapegoats for broader failures, breathe a sigh of relief. To achieve this shared sense of purpose, a few key technical lessons have come to light:

Establishing a clear call to action: It is critical to link the partnership's work to a clear and present local need. Unfortunately, this typically can't be solely about improving educational outcomes. Instead, we have found it often has to be linked to other issues such as economic development or civic improvements.

For example, in Albuquerque a group of partners had already come together to identify cities nationally that they held up as benchmarks for their community. All had higher college attainment rates. They saw this as a critical driver of the economic development results that eclipsed results in their own backyard. So they looked at their current baseline college attainment rates, set a concrete goal that would have them competing with these peer communities, and made this their call to action. In concrete terms, in order to stay competitive economically with these other communities, they need to achieve a college attainment rate of 50 percent, which means adding 60,410 graduates from some form of postsecondary education by 2020. That is their goal—not only to move forward on educational outcomes but also on the economic development goals of their region as a whole—a powerful call to action.

Embracing transitions: For far too long, major education reform has been tied to the engagement of individual leaders. As a result, people are hesitant to follow when a strong advocate for systems change emerges. In the back of their minds, they doubt it can last beyond an effective individual's inevitable departure. Instead of fearing such transitions, they should embrace them as opportunities. If trust has been built, new leaders can and will emerge. In Cincinnati and Northern Kentucky, when Nancy left, many thought the partnership would fade. Instead, other leaders stepped forward, and many felt it got stronger because there was clearly a sense of shared ownership for results.

Finding the right seat on the bus: Very early on, partners often focus solely on the leadership table necessary to champion this work. But that is only one small piece of the puzzle. There are a variety of other "tables"—action teams or committees—that need to be formed. These include data teams to help build the capacity of partners to utilize data, as well as Collaborative Action Networks to dig deep into the actions related to each of the partnership outcomes. Together, these tables become an interdependent ecosystem to move the dial over the long term. As Jim Collins called for in *Good to Great for the Social Sector*, we are not just getting people on the bus, we are working to get people in the right *seats* on the bus.

In order to help partners understand the importance of the various tables and their interconnectedness, there must be a way to convey this very early on in the work. Experiences from multiple sites teach us the importance of describing the structure as a network of networks with details about the role of each entity and how they interrelate. A concrete set of roles and responsibilities needs to be documented for each group. We have used a tool developed by Bain Consulting called RAPID—which stands for Recommend, Agree, Perform, Input, and Decide—to help communities with this difficult task. For each table in the accountability structure, communities identify the roles they play using this frame, and backbone staff make sure not to overstep these boundaries.

Visibly owning the outcomes—especially for the most vulnerable: The leadership of educational systems and institutions is often reticent to join these partnerships, especially when the early focus is on the agreement and sharing of outcome data. They flash forward to the day when they will have to stand up and publicly present data that may not always be flattering. This is completely understandable. District leaders in particular already have to face this annually when states report on test results. Why would they want to have to go through this again?

In reality, these leaders should not have to present the data alone. If we embrace shared accountability with differentiated responsibility, anyone in the partnership should be willing and able to share the data as if they were his or her own. In most communities, they hold an annual event around the release of the dashboard or report card of shared community-level outcomes. If business or philanthropic leaders present the data along with educational leaders and discuss how the collective body is working to move the results, it can build a shared ownership in a visible way.

This finding also underscores a critical priority around eliminating disparities. As Dan Ryan noted, Portland's All Hands Raised (AHR) partners have placed equity at the center of their efforts because, "We need to develop a mentality that the kids in *our* community are a *shared* responsibility. The hard truth is that we are failing far too many of our kids." By having multiple partners visibly demonstrate they feel a clear sense of ownership for outcomes, we also convey that the success of every child matters.

This commitment is particularly important for the most vulnerable. At the past two StriveTogether convenings, the broader network has raised the importance of talking about the issues of race and equity. As a result, we have developed a host of recommendations for communities to address this concern. Foremost among them is the commitment to disaggregate data. This means every community in the network must commit to pulling apart datasets by race at the community level and the programmatic level. This provides a critical picture to understand not only where the challenges lie but also drill down on which supports and interventions are most impactful for different populations. Albuquerque is a great example of the former, having undertaken geospatial mapping and setting a goal of eliminating the achievement gap as part of their partnership. And now they're taking the next step of digging deeply into programmatic data to understand what works for kids in these neighborhoods.

Building this sense of shared accountability and differentiated responsibility is never easy. A host of political issues will invariably get in the way.

Lesson Two: Clarity is critical

Unless all partners across sectors understand how decisions are made, the development of trust will not be on a solid footing. There are decision points early on that are particularly important when working to establish the core purpose of the partnership. These do not have to be finalized from day one. In fact, we recommend putting "draft" on every single document for weeks if not months to make sure you are able to capture and reflect as many voices as possible. But the key areas where clarity is needed include:

• Establishing the vision, mission, goals, and outcomes.

• Creating the accountability structure for managing the work.

• Selecting priority outcomes for initial focus.

In every case, it is critical for the partners helping to shape these items to set some criteria for how decisions are being made. These criteria should be shared again each and every time drafts are presented for consideration.

For example, in Cincinnati and Northern Kentucky the partnership lists the criteria used for selecting outcomes in every single report card. In fact, until we established these criteria with a group of respected local data experts, nobody could agree on outcomes. Once they were firmly established, it was possible to align around a common set of outcomes. You can find the complete list in the annual report card at www.strivepartnership.org, but it includes items such as the ability to collect data at the population level—with fidelity, in an affordable manner, and on a regular basis—and ensuring there is broad understanding of what the data point means. This level of transparency helps ensure that over time, people understand not only why the outcomes were selected but also the criteria that must be met to change the list in the future.

We have found that even with the criteria in place, a primary concern still remains about decisions being made in a "top-down" manner. Change theorist Michael Fullan (1993) has studied major change efforts in a broad spectrum of sectors, concluding that both top-down and bottom-up strategies are necessary to achieve transformational change:

> We have known for decades that top-down change doesn't work (you can't mandate what matters). Leaders keep trying because they don't see any alternative and they are impatient for results (either political or moral reasons). Decentralized solutions like site-based management also fail because groups get preoccupied with governance and frequently flounder when left on their own. Change flourishes in a "sandwich." When there is consensus above, and pressure below, things happen.[1]

Sites are working now to embrace community and expert voices as part of decision-making processes. Gwen Corley-Creighton in Richmond was emphatic in her comments about grassroots involvement:

> We are very concerned about authentic community engagement, because we know that as long as it's simply organizations and institutions coming and doing to and for the community, we'll only make small strides. Unless the community really *owns* and *guides* and *directs* the process, we're not going to get the kind of long-term impact we're trying to achieve of having productive citizens across the community. So we have a team that's focused on just that: Opportunities for Community Engagement. And it's not simply community representation. There's an authentic

relationship-building process that has to take place over time. You don't have bodies at a table simply to meet quotas or to represent groups. Those in the grassroots community must be able to speak and *drive* the process. This comes down to making sure that there's an intentional effort to identify what the strengths and the assets are in that community because we have a tendency to only focus on the problems, the challenges.

Framework Pillar II: Evidence-Based Decision Making

Two key lessons have emerged related to this pillar of the Framework: making sure partners are not derailed by letting perfect be the enemy of good when using data and the need to focus on data systems that connect actions to outcomes.

Lesson One: Don't let perfect be the enemy of good

In the early phases of this work, there is a temptation to try to get everything just right. This is particularly true when it comes to agreeing on outcomes. Since data have been used most often in the social sector for punitive purposes, there is a tremendous weight put on measures and how they should be used. In Cincinnati and Northern Kentucky, the debate over which outcomes to select raged on for more than a year. There were concerns that the measures were not consistent across the two states. Others feared that for certain measures, such as high school graduation rates and college completion rates, the calculations used did not reflect reality. At one point, we were not going to share any data until the metrics were the same in both states and the formulas were just right. Neither is true today. If we had waited, the StrivePartnership would not exist.

The president of Northern Kentucky University at the time, Jim Votruba, helped end this logjam when he stated, very simply, "We can't let perfect be the enemy of good." He argued that we would never get perfect data in the social sector, but that we had to be confident we would get better data over time and had to simply start with what we had, essentially stating that it may not be perfect, but it was better than nothing at all.

Another partner, Dean Larry Johnson from the University of Cincinnati, noted soon thereafter, "Good data will drive out bad data." We are seeing this happen. The two communities in Northern Kentucky eventually agreed on a single measure for early childhood that led to a better tool to understand progress. On the other end of the continuum related to college completion, a formula was developed to more accurately reflect college completion rates for students at community colleges. We are seeing partners embrace new and better ways of measurement over time. By starting with what we had, the community was able to foster a productive discussion about meaningful data rather than closed-door meetings that led to little or no progress on the ground.

We have seen across the country that sites are able to get agreement much more expeditiously than the founding cradle-to-career sites by keeping this mantra front and center: Don't let perfect be the enemy of good. And while using this to select community-level outcomes is critical early on, it becomes even more important as a site begins to think deeply about how to collect the necessary data to connect actions to outcomes.

Lesson Two: Connecting actions to outcomes

Once communities agree on community-level outcomes and priorities, the work to actually use data on the ground to begin to shine a light on success and uncover gaps really begins. In traditional strategic planning, the typical move at this point is to start new programs or launch an initiative. But in cradle-to-career work, it is all about having the discipline to look at local data first to learn from what is working on the ground. This usually uncovers a major outage: the sophistication of our data systems to connect action to outcomes.

Most communities have found ways to creatively report on outcomes at the community level so that the data are understandable and meaningful. In fact, StriveTogether created and open-sourced a tool to help with this process, which can consume significant time and resources. But even more important than the technology is clearly connecting what is being done on the ground to the outcomes we want to improve. Most communities require a deeper understanding of the connections between what happens in classrooms and improved educational outcomes. This is true at all levels, from early childhood to college. And as it relates to supports form nonprofits and social services, most of the data are related to inputs (such as how many kids are being served) as opposed to outputs (what happens to those kids as a result of the intervention).

If at all possible, we recommend that communities convene data teams at the outset of the process. This group includes partners who have access to data within and across systems as well as experts in how to use data for continuous improvement. Note that this is very different from traditional evaluation. Network members have had great success recruiting experts from hospitals, since the health sector is much more advanced in using data in real time for improvement. The corporate sector can also bring great expertise to bear.

The role of the data team goes beyond creating the annual dashboard or report card. They also support partners in developing the data management infrastructure needed to collect and analyze data. And they report back to networks of practitioners in a way that they can understand and apply the information effectively. As a partner at one site noted, "This is not fun or pretty, but there are few things more critical." In the end, if you don't have data on what is happening on the ground, there is no way to build on what works.

Seattle's Roadmap Project was the lead in developing one of the winning federal Investing in Innovation Fund (I3) grants in 2012. They received $30 million, more funding than any other applicant. A significant portion of these funds is being used to develop a comprehensive data management system with a new platform that pulls in existing data from other data systems. This investment will inform the field as a whole about how to overcome hurdles and create such technology systems as efficiently as possible. But even more important is the wide recognition among partners that this effort is worthy of the significant capital investment required to connect actions to outcomes.

Framework Pillar III: Collaborative Action

The two key lessons related to the third pillar of the Framework are grounded specifically in how to use data to inform work on the ground with children. This includes using data not just to *prove* what works but also to *improve* what partners are doing every day, as well as the importance of gaining momentum by building on bright spots.

Lesson One: Improve, not just prove

Aimee Guidera of the Data Quality Campaign has noted on many occasions that data in the social sector in general and education specifically are most often used as a "hammer instead of a flashlight." This means the culture around data utilization is one of fear and loathing. People assume data will be collected and reported to tell them if they won or lost; if they are good or bad. As a result, it takes considerable effort on the part of leadership to reinforce that instead of representing an annual dressing-down, data can actually be a flashlight that helps inform practice every day.

The importance of data, and of having the courage to *use* the data cannot be overstated. As Chad Wick noted,

> We are often too polite to go beyond looking at the data and ask the tough questions. "Where are our kids falling through the cracks? You know, we're almost always losing them in freshman math, or here, or there." But we haven't had the courage yet to ask, "What's going wrong in freshman math and what are we going to do to fix it?" The communities that do that are really jumping to the front of the pack and teaching us all something.

It is incumbent upon leadership to change this paradigm, creating a safe space where data can be used effectively rather than punitively. We recommend that key leaders—CEO-level executives engaged in the partnership—adopt a specific outcome they care about the most and engage with the practitioners working in networks to improve. If they are willing to attend meetings and dig into the data with people who work on the ground and model using data to improve, it can help dramatically to change the typical paradigm around data.

Investors have a particularly important role to play here. Private and public funders can significantly influence the way practitioners think by making learning part of their expectations. Instead of just asking in grant reports whether or not something worked, they can explore and ask what practitioners learned and how they applied that learning to improve. The signal this sends about the importance of using data to improve—not just prove—can rapidly accelerate success for cradle-to-career partnerships. The positive impact amplifies if investors continue putting resources behind work that may not have gotten expected results initially but where a solid plan was developed based on a thorough understanding of the data to drive improvement.

Portland modeled beautifully how to promote this proactive use of data through their Ninth Grade Counts initiative. As noted in chapter 4, a cross-sector group of partners came together and identified what was (1) causing dropouts after eighth grade as students transitioned into high school and (2) helping to reduce dropout rates. As a result of their efforts, students flagged as at risk of dropping out who participate in Ninth Grade Counts, when compared to nonparticipants, earned significantly more credits in ninth grade (six credits compared to five), met the crucial on-track-to-graduate benchmark (six credits or higher) at a 12 percent higher rate, and had better school attendance by 24 percent.

It is worth noting that we believe this use of data for continuous improvement is the next frontier of work that will move sites to proof point across the network. The lessons that are emerging from the field will give us an even stronger sense of what needs to be replicated.

Lesson Two: Build on the bright spots

To create a culture of embracing data to improve outcomes requires community leaders to identify and build upon early wins. In their wonderful book *Switch*, Chip and Dan Heath call these early wins "bright spots."[2] What are the wins you can build upon to build momentum? How do we demonstrate we are not starting from scratch—to directly shine a light not just on outages, but also on success we can build upon to thrive?

It is critical to note that the work does not stop once we identify these bright spots. It is actually just beginning. We continue to learn about applying the concepts of continuous improvement science, and more will emerge in the future. But we do know that when we get wins, we need to lift up the *practices* that led to improvement—not just the programs themselves. And then we need to work closely with practitioners to think about how quickly and effectively to scale what you've learned.

Seattle scored an early win related to the latter end of the educational pipeline: postsecondary success. They identified a scholarship that was highly undersubscribed and engaged seven districts to identify students who would be eligible. The Road Map Project regularly reported on how many of their students were actually applying over the course of several months. Not surprisingly, numbers shot up. Josh Garcia viewed the Road Map Project and its reporting of results as catalytic:

> The tremendous response to College Bound Scholarships is a classic example of how one expectation can rally seven different districts for a common cause and get results very quickly . . . Now, we still have to live up to that promise, but now we have kids signed up, kids aware, and how did that start? It was Mary Jean constantly saying, "Here's the progress," and it is really tied to what people want: their kids to be successful, to have that opportunity. It is not, "Wait a year for test results." It's "Here's our goal; here's the feedback continuously, and what are you *doing* about it?"

Framework Pillar IV: Investment and Sustainability

Two key lessons around Pillar IV have merged with resounding clarity as sites begin cradle-to-career collective impact work. The first is about the role of the "backbone" as described in the original *Stanford Social Innovation Review* article. But it's important to note, as described later, we see this as a function, not an organization. Second, sites must build on existing assets first to communicate to partners that this is not a new program, it's about a new way of doing business with existing resources.

Lesson One: Backbone or go home

The importance of a core central staff to help orchestrate the work of a cradle-to-career partnership operating in complex systems was brought home acutely on a recent site visit to help launch a partnership in Winston-Salem, North Carolina. After hearing about the fundamentals of collective impact, and delving into some details on how the work can be operationalized, one participant looked like she was in complete shock. When she eventually expressed her concerns, she stated the following, "I love this concept. But as an investor, I feel like I am being asked now to fund a data expert to work in each and every organization serving children in our community. My board just won't go for that."

This reaction speaks precisely to the centrality and power of the backbone organization. Instead of having to invest in an army of data analysts and experts to work in each organization individually, a centralized staff works to connect leaders and support the effective collection, management, and utilization of data across organizations. In fact, having a centralized resource that can work across organizations helps promote the alignment of organizations around outcomes and data management and tears down the silos and inefficiencies of isolated organizations.

As described in detail in the partnership staff profiles in chapter 2, we have found that there are four critical roles that simply must be played: Partnership Director, Data Analyst, Continuous Improvement Facilitator, and Communications/Community Engagement Manager.

While all four roles are critical, the importance of finding the right Partnership Director cannot be emphasized enough. Josh Garcia, a school administrator in the Seattle Roadmap Project, said the following about Mary Jean and her role as executive director:

> One thing that makes Mary Jean Ryan special is that she has connections with people from various sectors of our state, government and nongovernment, big city and small city, suburb, and so forth. They trust her; they like her and have seen her work over the years. I think her reputation and her background are why people have invested the amount of time this takes to succeed in this effort. I know I jumped at the opportunity.

One additional note related to this critical point: Describing the backbone as a *function* rather than a single organization can help partners see the big picture and not get stuck in the politics of selecting where the staff will land. The core staff roles do need to be housed in a central location, and they will help steer the partnership. But they alone cannot carry the weight of fundamentally changing the educational landscape of a given town, city, or region. Instead, there are a host of roles partners can play as part of this broader backbone function. These include convening and managing networks of practitioners around a given outcome, leading the work of the data team to help support the data analyst, or convening a policy and advocacy group to develop an agenda around the practices that get results for kids.

In Cincinnati, KnowledgeWorks agreed to house and support the core staff, which has created a strong home base for the StrivePartnership. But staff also work closely with the United Way of Greater Cincinnati to lead the work in early childhood and, with Cincinnati Children's Hospital Medical Center, to provide training in continuous improvement practice. A host of other partners play important roles—big and small—all of which are essential to the backbone function.

Once a site has been able to secure resources for the backbone, the partnership can turn its attention toward aligning local resources behind collaborative action plans for spreading and scaling what works. This brings us to our final lesson.

Lesson Two: Focus on existing assets first

In the early days of the StrivePartnership, we began to work with a specific group of five investors that were early adopters of this concept, the major players in town connected to grant making. Because those investors were with us every step of the way in the first year, we then made the assumption that what we had created—this process to use data to inform decisions—was so sound that other investors would welcome such an asset. So we tried to convene them around the concept of creating a pooled fund to support the backbone function and invest in practices that work.

This meeting, and a second similar attempt, landed with a thud. Not only did the other investors not feel engaged, they felt left behind. Based on the limited information they had received about the work, they believed that our primary goal was to influence existing resources rather than look for new funds. They were baffled and confused.

We had to take a step back and realize that this is not only a major shift for educators; it is a major shift for investors. That is why partnerships must work with both public and private investors one on one to (1) identify the outcomes they care deeply about, (2) understand what information would be most helpful to them to make more informed decisions, and (3) establish clear expectations for the timeline for the work and deliverables they could expect to emerge.

Identifying early wins or bright spots that model how to use existing resources differently is a big shot in the arm for investors, providing clarity about how to lay the groundwork for using the information provided by the backbone staff to inform future investments.

Ken Thompson of the Gates Foundation, who is working closely with the Road Map Project, has explained their work to engage funders. He notes,

> Alignment is a broad concept that funders can realize in lots of different ways. Our early approach has been about getting funders to come and discuss what alignment could mean. We need to understand how individual funder investments can best interact with each other, and be more thoughtful about how our current plans for investing make sense in combination with other investments. That idea has seemed to resonate well with funders in our community.

The Next Generation of Knowledge

These lessons are just scratching the surface of what is emerging within this rapidly growing field of collective impact generally and the work of building cradle-to-career civic infrastructure in particular. As more sites adopt the Theory of Action to guide their work, we will be able to identify which quality benchmarks have the most impact. And by winning big and failing forward, sites will be generating lessons related to each benchmark; so new sites will have the advantage of a growing body of evidence to guide their decisions and process.

The goal of StriveTogether and the Cradle to Career Network is to leverage the power of all the sites nationally to identify concrete lessons and share them in creative ways. The singular focus will be on expediting the progress of sites to become proof points. And to make sure this happens expeditiously, we will support sites to capture what they learn about quality collective impact and make it broadly available to the field as a whole.

SUCCEEDING TOGETHER
A Quick Guide to Creating Cradle-to-Career Civic Infrastructure

While each community's cradle-to-career civic infrastructure is unique, there are some key lessons from sites across the country that can help to expedite progress—aligned with the Four Pillars of the StriveTogether Framework.

 PILLAR I - SHARED COMMUNITY VISION

Community leaders across sectors own a common vision for the success of children and can communicate the outcomes and strategies to achieve it.

Shared Accountability, Differentiated Responsibility: Community partners respect the role they play in a broader ecosystem of activities to improve outcomes at scale.

Clarity is Critical: Partners consistently create clear and transparent criteria for how key decisions are made, and then outline their roles for implementing relevant action items.

 PILLAR II - EVIDENCE-BASED DECISION MAKING

Community partners agree on the outcomes they want to improve and build data systems designed to understand what works.

Don't Let Perfect Be the Enemy of Good: Data will never be perfect— but community partners can embrace the data they have and ensure the quality improves over time.

Connect Actions to Outcomes: Collect programmatic data along with outcome data to connect action on the ground—this is what enables communities to identify and build on what works.

 PILLAR III - COLLABORATIVE ACTION

Community partners are empowered with data on the impact of their work so they can work together to see improved outcomes.

Improve, Not Just Prove: Instead of a hammer, data should be used as a flashlight to lift up practices that can be spread across systems for greater impact.

Build on Bright Spots: Communities can build momentum by identifying success stories in their own backyard and finding creative ways to take them to scale.

 PILLAR IV - INVESTMENT & SUSTAINABILITY

Investors have put funds behind what works, community members own their roles, and backbone staff connect the dots necessary to scale success.

Backbone or Go Home: Establish a central backbone function that acts as the glue across the partnership, with a minimum of three key staffing roles in place.

Focus on Existing Assets First: Cultivate the discipline to focus on finding and building on what works at the outset—this will set a set the tone that it's not more "spray and pray."

CHAPTER 9

Striving Together

Critical Next Steps

StriveTogether's focus today is on expediting the development of cradle-to-career partnerships in communities across the country by facilitating knowledge-sharing among network members. The national Cradle to Career Network, along with the National Advisory Board and the implementation of the Theory of Action, make up a powerful set of models to inspire, inform, and advise new partnerships as they emerge.

Cradle-to-career sites that move across the Gateways in the Theory of Action to demonstrate real systems change will become the exemplars for this work. Together, these sites will:

- Continually assess and share progress using the Theory of Action.

- Refine the Theory of Action to establish standards of practice.

- Build the necessary local data management infrastructure to collect, analyze, and report data over time to show how civic infrastructure changes outcomes for children on the ground.

- Model a commitment to continuous improvement by sharing successes and failures related to how the partnership has applied learning in operations and implementation.

The network continues to emphasize its call for continued collaboration among the communities and partnerships that make up the national network. In our experience, the more these groups work together—both within their community and within the larger, national community—the more progress will be made in improving educational outcomes. And if communities model the concept of "failing forward," they will move forward in a humble way that enables others to grow and improve at an accelerated pace.

StriveTogether supports the Network's momentum by keeping members informed and providing them with open channels of communication. The StriveTogether website is becoming increasingly interactive, with portals both public and private that encourage discussion between networks and increase access to information, tools, and services. Each year, we host a national convening of network partners, where emphasis is again placed on sharing best practices and keeping each other apprised of the latest interventions and strategies at work across the country.

At the 2013 convening, in Dallas, Texas, member communities were required to sign the Commitment to Quality in order to remain a network member. As Jeff emphasizes to network members, the Theory of Action is the embodiment of the belief that we have to sustain quality and rigor. By signing the Commitment to Quality, sites are acknowledging that they have to meet these benchmarks. StriveTogether, meanwhile, is identifying those sites as the leaders who will define this field of collective impact and the practice of building civic infrastructure.

As a result of the high bar set by the Commitment to Quality, there is now an expectation that membership in the national network may decrease. Those who remain will be doing this work with the highest level of quality and will be dedicated to the hard work required for success.

StriveTogether has evolved from a concept sketched on a napkin after a challenging meeting in Cincinnati to a national network that informs federal education policy, restores vibrancy in communities across the country, and redirects the course of millions of children's lives in cities across America.

The impacts of this work can be most clearly seen in its birth community, where, in March 2013, the StrivePartnership of Cincinnati/Northern Kentucky's fifth annual report card was highlighted by an astounding 89 percent of the desired outcomes for student success trending upward. That is a considerable increase over previous years in which 81 percent of outcomes in 2011 and 74 percent of outcomes in 2010 were on the ascent. This is a dramatic proof point when one recalls the distressing and stagnant state of education in the region when Nancy was appointed president of the University of Cincinnati in 2002 and, together with Chad, Kathy, Rob, and many others, began putting the local education system back together.

Specifically, kindergarten readiness at Cincinnati Public Schools reached 55 percent in the 2012–2013 school year, an increase of 11 percentage points since the StrivePartnership's inception and its baseline data year of 2005–2006. In addition, first-to-second-year college retention has

> "The more we see of this effort, the more impressed we are. In fact, we believe it may be the most effective educational improvement in this region ever."
>
> —*Cincinnati Enquirer* Editorial Board, 2007

remained steady since 2005–2006 at two-year institutions and increased at four-year institutions. Cincinnati State Technical and Community College and Gateway Community and Technical College reached college retention rates of 56 and 67 percent, respectively, while Northern Kentucky University and the University of Cincinnati reached 65 and 86 percent, respectively.[1]

"The good news is that more kids are doing better," said Greg Landsman, executive director of the StrivePartnership. "But as a community, we need to own the fact that we have a long way to go. Together, we need to work harder to ensure every single child in our region succeeds."

The same can be said for the national network. As more communities across the country successfully meet the quality benchmarks outlined by the Theory of Action, their local impact will continue to gradually and collectively create a national system of education that achieves our ultimate goal: *supporting the success of every child, every step of the way, from cradle to career.*

Funding to Support the Backbone Entity in Collective Impact Efforts

In the article "Collective Impact," John Kania and Mark Kramer note this difficult work "requires a separate organization and staff with a very specific set of skills to serve as the backbone for the entire initiative."[1] We could not agree more and have found that communities that are able to fill the key staffing positions—an executive director and data analyst—as soon as possible in the process of building a partnership make significantly more progress. We have also found that while many acknowledge the necessity of having a backbone organization, fundraising for this critical function can often be a challenge.

The difficulty in raising funds is understandable: Funding for core operations (e.g., backbone support) is not likely one of the most attractive support options for funders when compared to investing in programs that directly serve children. As a result, effectively framing the value of the role is critical to ensure that collective impact efforts are sustained over time. The key messages we have found that can attract investors include:

- The reality that investing in programs alone rather than a very small amount of critical infrastructure has not led to the desired population-level impact we all so desire.

- The relative investment in the basic core staffing and related costs is remarkably small compared to the amount of existing resources that can be influenced. For example, in one community the backbone operating costs are $520,000, but the backbone directly influences over $4.5 billion when considering the resources represented at the partnership table.

- The efficiencies that will be realized by being more disciplined in using the data across similar partners far outweigh the limited investment in the backbone function.

All of these messages come back to a common and central tenet in collective impact: Cross-sector leaders can have greater impact by using data in a more disciplined way to inform decisions from the boardroom to the classroom.

Establishing the Value Proposition

In addition to identifying concrete messages that will resonate in your community to help build the case for the backbone, it's equally important to work with cross-sector partners to begin to highlight the roles of the backbone. Cross-sector partners need to help pinpoint the specific ways a backbone could contribute to the success of their organization and their sector. The needs of funders and service providers in particular—including practitioners in education systems, social services, and nonprofits—are critically important. Engaging these stakeholders early in the process specifically around the backbone role will help to both empower the staff and build support for investment.

Strategies for Fundraising for a Backbone Organization

After establishing the key messages and roles of the backbone, it is important to be very transparent with funders that the work of collective impact will require two different types of investment. Those funders who do not have an interest in funding the backbone organization need to understand they can still play a critical role in achieving collective impact. The second role they can play is around repurposing existing and investing new resources in the action plans that emerge around specific outcomes.

For those who are interested in funding the backbone, there are many options for generating a sustained funding stream to support the work over the long term. These options are meant as a starting place to generate a conversation that can lead to creative local solutions.

Potential Menu of Options for Funding the Backbone

Funding Opportunity	Example	Opportunities	Challenges
Align with partner(s)' strategic direction	Some United Ways and Community Foundations now consider acting as lead conveners.	Can connect the backbone's work to strategic plans of partners looking to try out this new role.	Organizations must be willing to cede strategy authority to the partnership table.
Segment funding to meet specific needs of the backbone:			
Funding to support data utilization	Resources to support data collection, deeper analysis for continuous improvement, design and distribution of annual report card, and data system development.	Creates high visibility for funders with report card and related media. Collecting data is critical component of achieving long-term outcomes.	Building data infrastructure and capacity is costly and needed for the long -term, so multiyear funding is often needed.
Funding for policy and advocacy	Salaries to support staff and consultants to translate programmatic work into policy recommendations; develop advocacy strategy.	Impact of policy change is long term.	Policy change is challenging to measure so outcomes may not be visible in the short term. Could be sensitivity around policy and advocacy, depending on the specific issue.
Funding for convening and engagement	Support for staff roles: executive director for alignment of partners; facilitators for action plan development; and organizers to mobilize around practices that get results.	Funders can be positioned as visionary for making the most visible investments for bringing key stakeholders together that have worked in silos over time.	Impact of improving student achievement takes time and can drain patience.
Funding to support backbone staff around specific outcomes	Identify funders with specific interests in a given outcome and ask them to support core functions, including staff costs, to champion that work.	Connects funders directly to a network and enables them to play a traditional funding role.	Funder must agree to let data drive the work rather than a specific strategy. Funder needs clear communications plan to invest in final plan.
Traditional campaigns	Nonprofits transitioning into this role often have traditional development plans, including events to support the core staff roles.	Leverages history— funders are comfortable with traditional approach.	Perception of competition with other providers; this can be mitigated by marrying funding for the backbone with action plan funds.

Published Reports That Discuss the StrivePartnership and StriveTogether

Bathgate, K., Colvin, R. L., & Silva, E. (2011). "Striving for student success: A model of shared accountability." Retrieved from http://www.educationsector. org/sites/default/files/publications/StrivingForStudentSuccess-RELEASED.pdf

Grossman, A. S., Lombard, A., and Fisher, N. (2014). "StriveTogether: Reinventing the local education ecosystem." Harvard Business School Publishing, Retrieved from http://hbsp.harvard.edu/he-main/resources/documents/web-files/314031p2.pdf

Hanleybrown, F., Kania, J., & Kramer, M. (2012). "Channeling change: Making collective impact work." *Stanford Social Innovation Review* blog, January 26. Retrieved from http://www.ssireview.org/blog/entry/channeling_change_making_collective_impact_work

Kania, J., & Kramer, M. (2011). Collective impact. *Stanford Social Innovation Review* (Winter). Retrieved from http://www.ssireview.org/articles/entry/collective_impact/

Park, S., Hironaka, S., Carver, P., & Nordstrum, L. (2013). Continuous improvement in education. Carnegie Foundation white paper. Retrieved from http://www.carnegieconnections.org/sites/default/files/carnegie-foundation-white-paper_2013_05.pdf

Philliber Research Associates. (2013). "Beyond content: Incorporating social and emotional learning into the Strive Framework." Retrieved from http://www.strivetogether.org/sites/default/files/images/Strive%20Together%20Volume%20I.pdf

Seldon, W., Jolin, M., and Schmitz, P. (2012). "Needle-moving community collaboratives: A promising approach to addressing America's biggest challenges."

Bridgespan Group Blog, February 6. Retrieved from http://www.bridgespan.org/getattachment/efdc40ca-aa41-4fb5-8960-34eb504eaf9a/Needle-Moving-Community-Collaborative-s-A-Promisin.aspxNOTES

StriveTogether. (2014). "Collective impact: Stronger results with community-based organizations." Retrieved from http://www.strivetogether.org/sites/default/files/images/CollectiveImpact_StrongerResultswithCBOs_2014.pdf

Additional Resources

All Hands Raised (Portland, OR): http://allhandsraised.org
All Kids Alliance (Houston, TX): http://www.allkidsalliance.org
Bridging Richmond (Richmond, VA): http://www.bridgingrichmond.org
FSG: http://www.fsg.org/
Living Cities: http://www.livingcities.org
New York State Cradle to Career Alliance: http://www.suny.edu/cradletocareer
Road Map Project (Seattle, WA): http://www.roadmapproject.org
StriveTogether Website: http://www.strivetogether.org
StriveTogether Blog: http://www.strivetogether.org/blog
StrivePartnership of Cincinnati/Northern Kentucky: http://www.strivepartnership.org

APPENDIX D

StriveTogether Cradle to Career Network Members

City	State	Partnership Name
Albuquerque	New Mexico	Mission: Graduate
Anchorage	Alaska	Anchorage United for Youth
Austin	Texas	E3 Alliance
Bellevue	Washington	Eastside Pathways
Boston	Massachusetts	Boston Opportunity Agenda
Charleston	South Carolina	Tri-County Cradle-to-Career Collaborative
Chicago	Illinois	Thrive Chicago
Cincinnati, Covington, Newport	Ohio/Kentucky	StrivePartnership
Columbia	Missouri	Columbia Cradle to Career Network
Columbus	Ohio	Learn4Life Columbus
Dallas	Texas	The Commit! Partnership
Quad Cities	Iowa/Illinois	Achieve Quad Cities
Dayton	Ohio	Learn to Earn
Decatur & Macon Counties	Illinois	Education Coalition of Macon County
Fresno	California	Fresno Area Strive
Grand Rapids	Michigan	KConnect
Green Bay	Wisconsin	Achieve Brown County
Itasca Area	Minnesota	Itasca Area Initiative for Student Success
Las Vegas	Nevada	Las Vegas Healthy Communities Coalition
Marin County	California	Marin Promise
Memphis	Tennessee	Strive Mid-South
Milwaukee	Wisconsin	Milwaukee Succeeds
Northeast	Indiana	Big Goal Collaborative
Northern (Shreveport)	Louisiana	Step Forward
Northfield	Minnesota	Northfield Promise
Norwalk	Connecticut	Norwalk ACTS
Phoenix	Arizona	Thriving Together
Portland	Oregon	All Hands Raised
Red Wing	Minnesota	Every Hand Joined
Richmond	Virginia	Bridging RVA
San Antonio	Texas	P16Plus Council of Greater Bexar County
San Diego	California	City Heights Partnership for Children
Santa Barbara	California	THRIVE Santa Barbara County
Sonoma County	California	Cradle to Career Sonoma County
South Seattle	Washington	The Road Map Project
Spartanburg County	South Carolina	Spartanburg Academic Movement
Spokane County	Washington	Excelerate Success
Summit County	Ohio	Summit Education Initiative
SUNY-Albany	New York	The Albany Promise
SUNY-Clinton County	New York	Clinton County THRIVE Partnership
SUNY-Rochester	New York	ROC the Future
Tacoma	Washington	Graduate Tacoma!
Toledo	Ohio	Aspire
Treasure Valley (Boise)	Idaho	Treasure Valley Education Partnership
Twin Cities	Minnesota	Generation Next
Washington	District of Columbia	Raise D.C.
Waterbury	Connecticut	Bridge to Success
Westbrook	Maine	Westbrook Children's Project
Winston-Salem	North Carolina	The Forsyth Promise

Notes

Introduction

1. Quoted in Carly Rospert, "What Is This Civic Infrastructure?" StriveTogether. org blog, http://www.strivetogether.org/blog/2012/08/what-is-this-civic-infrastructure/.

2. Jim Collins, *Good to Great for the Social Sectors* (New York: Harper Business, 2005), p. 1.

3. John Kania and Mark Kramer, "Collective Impact," *Stanford Social Innovation Review* (Winter 2011), http://www.ssireview.org/articles/entry/collective_impact/.

4. Kelly Bathgate, Richard Lee Colvin, and Elena Silva, "Striving for Student Success: A Model for Shared Accountability," *Education Sector Reports* (November 2011), p. 5.

5. Lucy Bernholz, "Philanthropy Buzzwords of 2011," Philanthrophy.com, http://philanthropy.com/article/Philanthropy-Buzzwords-of-2011/130151/

6. White House Council for Community Solutions, 2012 Final Report on Community Solutions for Opportunity Youth, http://www.serve.gov/sites/default/files/ctools/12_0604whccs_finalreport.pdf, page 13.

7. Jeff Edmondson, "The Difference between Collaboration and Collective Impact," *Striving for Change: Lessons from the Front Line*, http://www.strivetogether. org/blog/2012/11/the-difference-between-collaboration-and-collective-impact/.

Chapter 1. A Cincinnati Story

1. Gregory Korte, "How Cincinnati Got Segregated," Cincinnati.com, July 16, 2008, news.cincinnati.com/article/20080716/NEWS01/807160314/How-Cincinnati-got-segregated

2. Ohio History Central, http://www.ohiohistorycentral.org/entry.php?rec=681.

3. Cincinnati Public Schools, Districtwide Graduation Rate Data Review, www.cps-k12.org/home/GradRate.pdf.

4. StrivePartnership, 2008 StrivePartnership Report Card.

5. Dan Horn, "2001: A Timeline," *Cincinnati Enquirer*, December 30, 2001, www.enquirer.com/unrest2001/timeline.html.

6. Robert Greenleaf, *Servant Leadership: A Journey into the Nature of Legitimate Power and Greatness, 25th Anniversary Edition* (Mahwah, NJ: Paulist Press, 2002).

Chapter 2. Paving the Way for Quality Replication: A Framework for Cradle-to-Career Civic Infrastructure

1. StrivePartnership, 2012 StrivePartnership Report Card, http://www.strive-partnership.org/sites/default/files/wp-content/2012-13%20Partnership%20Report.pdf.

Chapter 3. Striving for Quality and Commitment: A Theory of Action

1. Jeff Edmondson, "The Difference between Collaboration and Collective Impact," *Striving for Change: Lessons from the Front Line*, http://www.strivetogether.org/blog/2012/11/the-difference-between-collaboration-and-collective-impact.

2. Jeff Edmondson, "The Impact Continuum: Recognizing the Value of Collaboration and Collective Impact," *Striving for Change: Lessons from the Front Line*, http://www.strivetogether.org/blog/2013/10/the-impact-continuum-recognizing-the-value-of-collaboration-and-collective-impact.

Chapter 4. Portland: All Hands Raised

1. Oregon Business Council, "A Check-Up on the Portland-Region's Economic Health," 2010, http://www.orbusinesscouncil.org/documents/portlandregioneconcheckup.pdf.

2. Portland Schools Foundation, *Connected by 25*, 2010 report, http://www.thinkschools.org/uploads/PSF_2PageCx25_April_20_2010Lo.pdf.

3. Address by Oregon governor John Kitzhaber to Cradle to Career Council, http://www.oregon.gov/gov/media_room/pages/speechess2011/cradletocareer_090911.aspx.

4. Attendance Works, The Chalkboard Project, and The Children's Institute and EcoNW, *Chronic Absence in Oregon*, a 2012 Oregon study.

5. SUN Service System Early Childhood Community Schools Linkage Project, 2010–2011 data. Chronic absence is defined as missing 10 percent of school or more.

6. Multnomah County Linkage Project, National Center for Community Schools report, "Chronic Absence in the Early Grades," data updated to 2010–2011 school year.

7. Portland Public Schools, 2009–2010 Milestones Update.

Chapter 5. Bridging Richmond

1. Bridging Richmond, "The Talent Dividend Initiative," November 2011, p. 31.

2. Ibid., p. 33.

3. Zachary Reid, "Central Virginia Partnership to Collaborate on Education," TimesDispatch.com, June 19, 2009, http://www.timesdispatch.com/news/central-virginia-partnership-to-collaborate-on-education/article_b28b18f5-6195-592f-845f-537249e5ffe6.html.

4. Smart Beginnings Greater Richmond Leadership Council, *Regional Plan for Children's Readiness*, http://www.yourunitedway.org/sites/yourunitedway.org/files/images/SB_School_Readiness_Plan_as_of_05_01_10.pdf.

Chapter 6. Seattle/South King County: The Road Map Project

1. Road Map Project, Annual Results Report 2012, http://www.nxtbook.com/nxtbooks/cced/2012annualreport/#/10.

2. Ibid.

Chapter 8. Lessons from Winning Big and Failing Forward

1. Michael Fullan, *Change Forces: Probing the Depths of Educational Reform* (London: Routledge, 1993), p. 37.

2. Chip Heath and Dan Heath, *Switch: How to Change Things When Change Is Hard* (New York: Crown Business, 2010).

Chapter 9. Striving Together: Critical Next Steps

1. http://www.strivepartnership.org/sites/default/files/wp-content/2012-13%20 Partnership%20Report.pdf.

Appendix A. Funding to Support the Backbone Entity in Collective Impact Efforts

1. John Kania and Mark Kramer, "Collective Impact," *Stanford Social Innovation Review* (Winter 2011), http://www.ssireview.org/articles/entry/collective_impact/.

Index